STRAIGHTFORWARD GUIDES

BAILIFFS AND THE LAW

DAVID SWAN

Straightforward Guides
www.straightforwardco.co.uk

Straightforward Guides
Brighton BN2 4EG

British Library Cataloguing in Publication Data. A CPN record of this book is available from the British Library.

ISBN 1 847160 61 1
9781847160614

Cover design by Bookworks Islington

Printed by Biddles Limited Kings Lynn Norfolk

BAILIFFS POWERS AND THE LAW

CONTENTS

Introduction

The use of bailiffs to seize goods in order to enforce unpaid debt is probably the commonest way of forcing individuals to satisfy their liabilities.

There are currently a number of forms of distress actively in use, enforced by different types of bailiff, with the law for each form of distress different. There are, however, various common principles running through every form of bailiff's action which we will look at throughout this book.

The Tribunals Courts and Enforcement Act 2007
This Act, which deals with reform of the tribunal system in the United Kingdom, and also with reform and amendment of the bailiff service, has been partially implemented at the time of writing. However, Part 3, which deals specifically with taking control of goods, has yet to be implemented. Although May 1st 2008 was the projected date, such has been the uproar over the proposed changes that no date is yet tabled.

The law will provide for a new system of taking control of goods in order to enforce judgements and will also abolish ancient common law writs and remedies such as replevin, fieri fascias and distress for rent (all of which you will encounter in this book). The new Act will also abolish the ancient office of bailiff and replace it with a modern system of certified enforcement agents. Other more minor changes will be made in parts 4-6.

Human Rights Act 1998
The Human Rights Act 1998 made the rights contained in the European Convention on Human Rights (ECHR) directly accessible through the local courts in England & Wales and,

although the UK has been required to adhere to these principles for many years, has inevitably refocused attention upon individuals' rights and the duties of public authorities.

The Act requires public bodies to respect citizens' human rights. The duty will extend to the bailiffs employed by public bodies. Two rights in the ECHR, the right to respect for the home (article 8) and the right to undisturbed enjoyment of possessions (first protocol, article 1) are most likely to impinge upon bailiffs' activities. However it is important to stress that the European Court of Human Rights in Strasbourg has made it clear that it sees no breach of human rights in the lawful use of bailiffs to enter property and seize goods.

National Standards for Enforcement Agents

The Government introduced a code of National Standards for Enforcement Agents (NSEA) in 2002 with which all bailiffs must now comply. It is required that copies of the NSEA Code must be freely available from the offices of enforcement agencies, from agents on request and wherever possible from creditors. The code is concerned with:

- The levying of distress by bailiffs:
- The business conduct of bailiffs
- The conduct of the creditor

In particular bailiffs organisations are required to be fully aware of their own responsibilities, which is likely to mean their liability for their bailiffs' actions and their duty to identify vulnerable individuals and deal with them accordingly.

Enforcement agents and creditors are reminded that they each have a role in ensuring that the vulnerable and socially excluded are protected. The recovery process should therefore include procedures to identify and deal appropriately with such individuals. Agents have a duty to contact the creditor and report the circumstances in situations where there is potential cause for concern. The standard states that those who might be potentially vulnerable include:

- elderly people;
- people with a disability and those suffering from serious illness;
- those recently bereaved;
- single parent families and pregnant women;
- unemployed people; and,
- those who have obvious difficulties with English.

All bailiffs' trade and professional bodies, central government departments and local authority associations have endorsed the NSEA therefore any failure to follow its provisions should be the subject of a complaint to both the bailiffs and the creditor.

1

Acting Before the Bailiff Arrives-Preventative Measures

Challenging alleged liability

The enforcement may be prevented if the debt can be challenged. This will remove any right to seize goods. The ability to challenge the debt will vary from debt to debt, as will the method of challenge to be employed.

Judgments

If a court judgement is being enforced by execution, it may be possible to challenge it if the judgment debtor did not respond to the initial claim form. If he did defend the case, and was unsuccessful, this opportunity has gone. If he failed to receive the claim form or did not deal with it, the chance to fight the case is not lost. It will be necessary to make application to the relevant court to have the judgment 'set aside'- or cancelled. The court will do this where there is both a good reason for failing to respond the first time and a defence to the claim which should be heard. If the person is liable, but cannot afford to clear the debt at once, this is not a defence. They should apply to 'stay' (or freeze) the execution. If, however, there is a valid basis upon which the claim may be contested- for instance a dispute as to liability or a counterclaim for damages, perhaps arising out of faulty goods or services, an opportunity will be given for these matters to be heard. Application is on court form N244 and there is a fee to pay. The application to set aside will be heard by the court and in the meantime the person should request that execution is stayed to prevent the bailiff taking any further steps. If the judgment is set aside there will no longer be a debt that the court can enforce, and a further hearing will follow to consider the claim and defence.

Liability orders

Local tax debts and arrears of child support maintenance are enforceable by distress once the council or CSA have obtained a Liability Order from the magistrate's court. This confirms the individual's liability for the unpaid debt. Issues of liability should be taken up not with the court but initially with the creditor, who, if the challenge is successful, should be invited to cancel or withdraw the order made. Some disputes may have to go to a special tribunal for a decision.

Road traffic orders

The county court order that must be obtained prior to the use of bailiffs is more like a liability order than a normal county court judgment. The procedure for imposing the penalty is as follows. Where an individual contravenes parking regulations a parking attendant employed by the borough can impose a penalty charge and may either fix notice of this on the car or give it to the driver. If the owner does not pay in 28 days notice is served on him/her by the local authority stating that there are a further 28 days in which to pay and that the charge will increase thereafter. If the person does not pay then a "charge certificate" is issued and the penalty increases by 100%. After a further fourteen days the local authority may apply to the county court for an order that it may recover the penalty as if it were payable under a county court judgment.

The debtor can challenge the original penalty charge notice after receiving it, on grounds such as the fact that he was not driving the car or that the car was no longer their property. He may later challenge the court order, on the grounds either that he did not receive the notice or that representations against it were ignored, by means of a statutory declaration. The effect of the declaration is to revoke any county court order and cancel any charge certificate. Standard forms for this purpose may be obtained from the county court.

Magistrates orders

The magistrate's court may use distress to impose a range of orders, though it will typically only be encountered being used to collect arrears on fines and other orders associated with criminal offences. Once the decision has been taken to use distress, it can be difficult to reverse that. The only other way of challenging the remedy through the court would be to attack the original conviction upon which it is based. This may involve appeal to either the Crown Court or High Court.

Other forms of distress

In every other case no involvement with the court is required and the decision that the debtor is liable and that distress should be used is solely a matter for the creditor. In such cases any challenge to liability will therefore have to be addressed to them directly.

Taxes

For unpaid income tax or VAT a process of appeal exists. It is usually possible to appeal late, if good reasons can be shown for the delay. Permission to do this may be needed from the tax collector or, if this is refused, from the appeal tribunal. Income tax liability is determined by the General Commissioners, and VAT is dealt with by a VAT Tribunal. Both are panels of lay experts who meet locally to hear and determine such cases. Details of the appeal process and the necessary forms may be obtained from the local tax office. The HMRC (Her Majesty's Revenues and Customs) bailiffs may be ordered to abandon the levy if the firm deregisters for VAT during the levy process.

Rent

If the problem is rent, the only course of action may be to take up the matter directly with the landlord. Private landlords of business premises and local authority and housing association landlords of 'secure' tenants may use distress without any prior warning although in the case of housing association tenants there is usually an involved procedure which takes place before any court actions.

Private commercial landlords may be more of a problem to negotiate with as they will have few qualms about the use of the remedy, nor may they be particularly flexible about rates of repayment.

Landlords of assured and protected tenants may only use distress having obtained permission from a county court in advance.

To be entitled to distrain, there must be rent in arrears to the landlord on a current tenancy. Distraint cannot therefore be used if the tenancy has been terminated by forfeiture, by a court order or by a notice to quit. Distress also cannot be used if new premises have been let to a tenant; if a new lease has been granted or if court action has been commenced.

Service charges, water, fuel and insurance may be recovered by distress only if they are treated as rent by the lease or tenancy agreement e.g. it describes them as being 'reserved' or 'recoverable' as rent. If the agreement includes such items as part of the rent payable, the landlord can distrain for the whole balance due. The arrears must be certain, so if a service charge treated as rent is variable, the sum due must have been agreed by the tenant or otherwise confirmed (e.g. by tribunal). It may also be possible for the tenant to set off against the arrears a claim for damages for disrepair. The claim may be raised at the hearing for permission, or if there is none or the debtor is too late for this, an injunction may granted to restrain a levy where the damages claim exceeded the rent due. Confronted with such a claim of disrepair, the bailiff can only take a provisional levy and refer back to the landlord.

Negotiation with a creditor

It is frequently the case for the bailiff to be instructed to collect the debt in a relatively short period of time. This will necessitate demands for the debt to be paid by high instalments. In some cases instruction to the bailiff is to refuse anything but a lump sum payment of the total debt. Where the debtor is on benefit or other low income, or has other personal or financial problems that may make such payment impossible negotiation with the creditor should be possible. The creditor should then be expected to tale payment directly and to withdraw the warrant from the bailiffs.

Suspending warrants

In some circumstances it is possible to stop the bailiff by application to the relevant court.

High Court stays of execution

Removal and sale of goods can be prevented by the defendant by applying for a 'stay of execution'. This can either be done soon after receiving the original claim form which demanded payment of the debt from the debtor or as soon as the sheriff has levied. The court can stay execution if there are special circumstances which indicate that the judgment should not be enforced or if it appears that the applicant is unable for any reason to pay. In such cases the court may stay the execution of the order either absolutely or subject to such conditions as it thinks fit. Application is on the general notice of application (form N244) and should be accompanied by a statement of income and expenditure and assets, preferably sworn on affidavit form N265. A fee is payable for the application.

Suspending county court execution

Preventing execution is a relatively straightforward process for the defendant in the county court. It involves completion of court form N245, the application to suspend the warrant. At the same time an offer of repayment can be made, varying the existing instalment order if necessary, and the form allows a person to supply considerable detail of their income, expenditure and other liabilities in order to back up any offer. A court fee is payable by the defendant when the application is filed.

Permission of court in distress for rent

A private landlord must obtain permission of the county court to use distress against a protected or statutory tenant under Rent Act 1977 or an assured or assured shorthold tenant under Housing Act 1988. At the hearing of this request the court has powers to adjourn, stay or postpone proceedings. Permission should not be granted if there is a dispute as to the rent due. The court has absolute discretion in deciding whether or not to grant permission, therefore it is possible to suspend the order on conditions such as weekly payment. Permission is also needed to levy against certain members of the armed forces.

Postponement of issue by magistrates

The court can postpone the issue of a warrant until such time and on such conditions as it thinks just. Applications for postponement may be made as often as necessary. The decision of the court to postpone will be made at the hearing at which it is ordered that the sum due be recovered by the use of distress.

If instalments under an order are in default, the court will issue enforcement for all instalments still unpaid. If the court imposing the fine allowed time to pay or set instalments, or if the defendant was absent at the hearing, distraint cannot be issued until the clerk has served notice in writing stating the total balance due, the instalments ordered and the date for payments to begin. Generally, a final demand will be issued and a warrant may be issued upon continued default.

At this hearing the court may require evidence of the existence of distrainable goods. If the evidence reveals a 'reasonable likelihood' that there are distrainable assets, a warrant *should* be issued. The use of distraint as an option and the availability of seizable goods should be considered before committal is threatened. In every case the defendant should have an opportunity to make representations at a hearing before the warrant is issued and thus there is a chance for distraint to be further postponed on varied terms of payment. The only exception to the debtor's right to attend is where the person is in prison, though there should still be a hearing.

However there is no power to postpone a warrant once it has been issued, nor is there any specific power to *suspend* warrants after they have been issued, unlike the civil courts.

Although the courts may not intervene to suspend a warrant, bailiffs have been given the power to do something similar. If a scheme of instalment payment can be negotiated with a person, the bailiff can get the court to approve a delay in the sale of goods seized for up to 60 days.

Protecting goods

If the liability cannot be disputed or the warrant cannot be stopped, the distress may still be defeated by depriving the bailiff of anything that may be seized. There are a number of means by which this can be done. One is by transferring goods to relatives, children or friends to put them beyond the reach of bailiffs. In genuine cases, if a third party then removed his/her goods before distress, they could not be sued. Two particular methods have been tried by debtors over the years and are described below. Simpler, more direct methods, may also be tried.

Bills of sale

These are effectively mortgages on goods. In return for a minimum loan of £30 from a third party (who may of course be a friend or relative) a person gives his/her possessions as security. Various formalities and procedures must be exactly followed for bills to be effective against bailiffs- these include the way the bill is drawn up and its registration in the High Court. Non-compliance with these rules will mean that the bill will be void and that the goods are not protected.

The effectiveness of a bill differs according to the debt being enforced by distress:

Execution

This cannot be levied on mortgaged goods and interpleader can protect the goods if this happens (see later chapter). If interpleader is begun by the mortgagee (the person who lent the money) the court will normally order sale of the goods and divide the proceeds.

Magistrates court

Distraint is prevented on mortgaged goods.

Local tax

Distraint on mortgaged goods is prevented.

Income tax

Distraint may proceed as normal.

Rent distress

This is not prevented, unless a Consumer Credit Act 'default notice' has been served by the mortgagee. This is in a form laid down by the consumer credit legislation and demands payment of the debt, or arrears, within a set period. However the mortgagee could remove the goods without it being fraudulent, for which see below.

Furniture leases

Another approach that is fairly common, especially amongst small firms, is for the debtor to transfer his/her assets to a friend or relative and then lease or rent the items back again, usually at a nominal rate of payment. Although distress for rent would not be prevented by this technique if the transfer were to a spouse or business partner (as the landlord's basic right is to seize *anything* found at the rented property) in most other cases it should be effective. However the courts may regard these arrangements as simply ways to avoid legal enforcement and refuse to uphold them in any action brought by the debtor for wrongful interference following seizure, just as with bills of sale above.

Hiding goods

There is nothing to stop the debtor hiding goods around his her home before the bailiff calls. It is not an offence and as most bailiffs do not search with any great diligence or thoroughness, it may be successful.

Removing goods

Along the same lines as the above, the debtor may pre-empt a bailiff's call by removing valuable items from the property. This is, in most cases, legal and will achieve the desired results. Even though most bailiffs may levy anywhere that goods may be found in England & Wales, in most cases they will of course be unable to find out where else items might be located, only having the debtor's home address. In execution the sheriff's officer or county court bailiff may pursue goods if they have been removed to third party premises to put them beyond his reach. The bailiff may also break into the third party's house in such cases. Demand for entry should be made first but force may then be used if entry is refused.

In distress for rent there is an offence called 'fraudulent removal'. This occurs when a tenant deliberately removes goods in order to defeat a levy of distress, leaving insufficient goods for distress behind. The landlord can pursue goods fraudulently or clandestinely removed within thirty days of their removal if they have not been sold in good faith and entry may be forced during day time to any premises if the landlord has grounds to suspect that fraudulently removed goods are inside (though a police officer should be present).

There can also be court proceedings for fraudulent removal. The tenant, and any person knowingly assisting, may be ordered by a county court to pay double damages to the landlord or a magistrates court can order a penalty of double damages which is payable as a fine.

2

Self-help Remedies

The fundamental principle exists in law that where an unlawful act is done against a person, they have the right to resist. Thus wrongful seizure of goods may be prevented by seizure back of those goods, termed 'rescue'. Equally wrongful entry to premises may be resisted by the use of reasonable force. Whilst forcible recapture and forcible resistance to wrongful seizure are lawful, the level of force that is permissible may be difficult to determine.

There are limits on how far self-help may go. The debtor may find that he has committed an offence in seeking to defeat the bailiff's lawful activities.

Contempt

A debtor may be guilty of criminal contempt if s/he obstructs a civil court bailiff in the execution of their duty. Obstruction includes assault and retaking seized goods. The bailiff can arrest the person and the court may commit or fine the offender.

It is contempt of court to interfere with the sheriff's officer whilst executing a writ or to take goods out of custody. If a sheriff's officer is resisted, he may arrest and imprison the guilty parties. The county court may commit and/ or fine any person who assaults an officer whilst in execution of his duty. The bailiff may arrest the offender without a warrant and take him /her before the judge, though he/she should be given full details of the allegations against them and given an opportunity to prepare a defence, seek legal advice and apply for legal aid. It would be a defence to say that the debtor honestly, but mistakenly, believed the victim was not a court officer or not acting in execution of his duty.

Forcible ejection
Using violence and threats of violence to eject a bailiff from premises which have been legally entered can lead to forced re-entry by the bailiff and possible prosecution of the debtor for assault. The person can be fined or imprisoned up to two years.

Interference with seized good
There are (in theory) two separate wrongful acts that can be committed by the debtor- rescue and poundbreach. The latter is most likely to occur, though the offences are often referred to simply as rescue. Each is both an offence for which the person may be prosecuted *and* a civil wrong for which the bailiff may claim damages. It is a defence for the debtor to say that the bailiff had seized goods illegally.

Criminal offences
Poundbreach is interference with impounded goods and is the offence most likely to be committed in these days of walking possession agreements. Such interference is an offence, whether or not there is a breach of the peace. The offender can be prosecuted and on conviction the sentence may be committal for an unlimited period or a fine of an unlimited amount, though it is usually based on the person's means and the gravity of the offence.

There are also specific criminal remedies:

Section 92 County Courts Act 1984
This states that any person rescuing seized goods is liable to prison of one month and/or a fine up to £2500. Arrest will either be on

the spot if they are caught by the bailiff though the person should be given full details of the allegations against them and given an opportunity to prepare a defence, seek legal advice and apply for legal aid. Alternatively proceedings may begin following a claim form from the court.

In magistrates court

If the bailiff levies upon household goods, they cannot be removed from the house before the day of the sale without the person's written consent but must instead be impounded with a conspicuous mark. It is an offence, punishable by fine, to remove the goods or remove or deface the mark

Civil claims

There is a civil remedy for poundbreach, which is to sue for damages. There are also specific remedies for different debts:

Landlords

Landlords may claim a penalty of treble damages for both rescue and poundbreach in the county court. The basis upon which the damages are calculated is the value of the goods seized.

The VAT Act 1994

Under this Act there is a civil penalty for breach of any walking possession agreement of fifty percent of the VAT due. The debtor will not be liable if he can convince the Commissioners or, on appeal, a VAT Tribunal, that there is a reasonable excuse for the breach. In such cases where an offence is alleged, arguments can arise as to whether poundbreach or rescue have indeed occurred and these will involve questions as to whether impounded goods have been abandoned or were properly impounded in the first place. There will be no abandonment, and therefore an offence will have been committed, where possession is adequately retained or the bailiffs *intends to retain* it. However no offence is committed by a person where goods are removed *after* the offence has been committed by another or where an innocent third party removes goods, unaware that they are subject to walking possession- for example another member of the debtor's family has moved goods or a hire firm recovers its property because rental payments are due.

Payment of a debt in full

Payment of the debt in full before the bailiff levies will terminate the process. If payment is made before seizure, the levy is illegal.

Becoming insolvent

The insolvency of the debtor has a major impact on the ability of the bailiff to proceed and will generally be a complete bar on any further progress with a levy. Though it is a desperate measure, in context of insurmountable debts, insolvency may be a solution.

Most insolvency procedure is laid down by the Insolvency Act 1986 and Insolvency Rules 1986, as amended by the 2002 Enterprise Act. These provide a code for the insolvency of individuals and lay down procedures to be followed in administering their affairs. Part of the work of administering insolvency falls to the courts and part lies outside the court system in the hands of the Official Receiver and private administrators known as Insolvency Practitioners (IPs). Both of these may be encountered as trustees of bankrupts.

The primary role of trustees is to realise the assets of the insolvent person and pay the debts. These are paid in a strict order: first secured creditors (such as mortgages), then the fees of the IP and/ or the Official Receiver, thirdly the 'preferential debts' such as VAT and National Insurance contributions, and finally, all other debts. Besides bankruptcy and individual voluntary arrangements provided for by the Insolvency Act, a person can also seek an Administration

Order in the county court. The legislation relating to this is found in the County Courts 1984 Act and County Court Rules 1981. Although as a result this may seem to be a purely civil court procedure, its origin is in the Bankruptcy Act 1883 and it is often termed the 'small bankruptcy'.

- *Individual Voluntary Arrangements* The Insolvency Act, as amended by the 2002 EA, introduced a new way for individuals to resolve financial difficulties-the individual voluntary arrangement (IVA). This enables a person who is in debt or facing insolvency to agree with their creditors proposals for the reorganisation of their finances in order to be able to avoid being made bankrupt. Creditors are offered a scheme of repayment that should leave them better off than if the person went bankrupt, and the debtor avoids all the stigma and restrictions of actually being an un-discharged bankrupt. IVAs can only be set up with the help of an Insolvency Practitioner and this can often make them too expensive for many people. However they have the advantage that enforcement is effected at two stages.

  \- *Interim Orders*: the initial stage of the procedure is for the debtor to formulate repayment proposals with the IP who acts as 'nominee' and draws up a detailed scheme for presentation to the creditors. To buy time for this work to be done, the debtor can apply to the court for an Interim Order. The Order lasts for fourteen days initially and its effect is that *"no execution or other legal process may be commenced or continued against the debtor or his property except with the permission of the court."*.

  The interim order will prevent seizure as follows:

  \- *execution* by civil court bailiffs is specifically stayed;

- *magistrates courts* would probably need permission of the bankruptcy court to issue any distraint warrant;

- *local taxes and child support maintenance:* it would seem that the making of the initial Liability Order needed for local tax and child support enforcement would require permission of the bankruptcy court. This being the case distraint may be prevented as a result of the need for a Liability Order.

- *Creditor's meeting*- before the expiry of the Interim Order the nominee must report to the court whether a creditors' meeting should be summoned to consider the IVA. If the court is satisfied from the report that the debtor has a scheme likely to satisfy his creditors the order is extended to permit the creditors to meet. The nominee sends details to all creditors and invites them to meet to vote upon the proposals. If seventy five per cent by value accept the scheme it comes into effect and all unsecured creditors are bound by it. This means that they *must* accept the repayments and cannot enforce their debts whilst the IVA is in force and the debtor is complying. As a consequence, no further bailiff action will be possible.

- *Bankruptcy* is begun by the presentation of a 'petition' either by the debtor or by a creditor. As long as at least £750 is owed almost any creditor may present a petition- VAT and income tax are common examples. Unpaid fines or maintenance may not form the basis of a petition. If the court is satisfied that a debt is due and that the debtor is unable to pay, a bankruptcy order will be made. A debtor may petition if he feels unable to satisfy his debts, whatever the total sum due but the major drawback of this is the cost-

presently nearly £300. Usually a bankruptcy order is made on such applications.

The making of a bankruptcy order has a number of effects on the person's finances and property, largely taking away the person's control of their affairs and placing the administration in the hands of a trustee, whose main job is to seek to raise what money can be recovered from the bankrupt's estate- his assets and income- in order to pay the creditors. However, in return, debtors are given substantial protection from enforcement by their creditors.

- *Pending petitions* Whilst a petition is pending the bankruptcy court may, on application from the debtor, stay any action, execution or legal process against his property or person (e.g. prevent an arrest or seizure of goods). Equally the court where the case is taking place, for instance a magistrate's court dealing with a Liability Order application, may stay proceedings or allow them to continue on terms.

- *Effect of order* After a bankruptcy order is made no creditor whose debt is included in the bankruptcy may take *any* steps against the person or property of the bankrupt. Property includes goods, chattels and money. The effect of this is to completely bar enforcement of an existing debt. These restrictions on enforcement are however subject to special rules applying to distraint and execution.

If new debts arise the situation is more complex. If there are no existing debts included in the bankruptcy then the creditor can proceed as normal except that the bankrupt can apply to stay enforcement in the same manner as described for pending petitions. In most cases there may be little reason to bar enforcement as bankruptcy does not absolve a person of responsibility for ongoing or subsequent liabilities. However if the creditor already has a debt included in the bankruptcy, permission of court is required to pursue any debt arising later.

- *Execution* Special provisions are made for the sheriff's officer and county court bailiff levying execution for any debt, whether provable or not. There must be an execution in progress for the provisions to apply- it must not have been withdrawn, completed or otherwise abandoned, for instance due to there being no available goods.

Where the execution was issued before the bankruptcy order was made but the process has not yet been completed by sale of goods (or by receipt of the proceeds of their sale), the creditor must abandon the seizure and is not entitled to retain any sums paid to avoid the execution. If the execution is complete, the claimant may retain the money regardless of the bankruptcy. The onus is on the creditor to prove that the execution had been completed, but a debtor may often need to raise the issue with them and draw it to the attention of the trustee as well.

An execution is not complete where:
- the bailiff has withdrawn upon agreeing instalment payments (as is commonly the case);
- the sheriff has withdrawn permanently with the creditor's consent on payment of a lump sum; or,
- the debtor pays the debt direct to the creditor.

Where any of the above apply the bankrupt may expect to be protected from the bailiff taking any further steps.

- *Distress for rent* There is a limited right of distress for a landlord. Generally rent arrears are unenforceable and will be included in the bankruptcy like every other debt of the tenant. However the landlord may distrain for rent due, but only for the six months immediately prior to the beginning of the bankruptcy, i.e. the date when the order was made. If there are no goods or where distress follows the petition anything other than the six-month's element must be included in the bankruptcy and cannot be the subject of distress.

The protection against the landlord's distress offered by the bankruptcy interestingly extends after discharge. Even then, the landlord cannot distrain upon any of the goods that were comprised in the bankrupt's estate.

- *Other distraint* None of the restrictions affecting landlords apply to other forms of distraint. Bailiffs may therefore proceed to levy against a bankrupt for local taxes, road traffic penalties and the like as normal. It is understood that HM Revenue and Customs will not exercise their rights to levy unless the debtor continues to trade and incurs further debts or if other creditors also continue to exercise their rights to levy, to the Revenue's possible detriment. For other creditors how to instruct the bailiffs is a matter of policy and certainly many local authorities do choose to continue with levies.

- *Administration Orders* Administration Orders are a county court procedure that permit debtors to consolidate all their debts into one total sum that is then administered for them by the court, which distributes affordable payments to all the creditors. Two conditions must be satisfied in order for a defendant to be able to apply:

-he/she must have at least one county court or High Court judgment entered, and have total debts of less than £5000.

If the order has been made it has a number of effects, such as freezing any interest that may be accruing on the debt, but the most important for our purposes is the consequence for bailiffs.

- *Enforcement* Once the order is made no creditor included on the order can take any action against the debtor except with permission of the court and on such terms as may be imposed. Notably this also applies to any creditor initially listed on the debtor's application, even though their debt is not subsequently included in the order because the court decided that it should be excluded. These creditors too will need permission of court before being able to enforce even though they are not being paid through the Administration Order. This will particularly effect local taxes and fines which are often excluded after objections by the local authority or magistrates court.

- Finally when any county court is notified of an administration order application by another court, proceedings against the person in that court are stayed.

- *A landlord* may still distrain for rent arrears due after an administration order has been made. The rent recoverable is however restricted to an amount of six month's rent due immediately before the date that the order was made and any other sums due may not be collected by distress- instead the landlord will have to claim for this surplus by entering a claim in the administration order.

3

The Bailiff's Visit

Final warnings

There will have been at least some contact from the creditor before the decision to enforce is made. The purpose of this is both to give warning and also to give the person a last opportunity to arrange payment. The nature and amount of warning given will depend on the debt due.

- *VAT:* A business will be given warning of the intended enforcement and an opportunity to pay. However because of the nature of the tax (i.e. crown revenue collected by the trader) HM Revenue and Customs will proceed to enforcement quite quickly. The process normally begins with the issue of an internal 'distress advice' that distraint may be necessary. This happens in three circumstances: where a VAT return is received without full payment; where the due date for any payment has passed and the debt is over £200; or where an assessment indicates that a debt of over £200 may be due. Assessments of tax are made if a registered person fails to make a complete return, or supply information required by HMRC. When notified to a person this assessment is treated as tax due and recoverable, but may be replaced at any time by a properly declared return. At this stage HMRC will normally try to negotiate. If this fails a 'demand notice for immediate payment' is issued. No time to respond to the demand notice is laid down in law, and it is at the local office's discretion though HMRC must wait thirty days after notification of an assessment before executing a warrant, unless the assessment has been notified in the absence of a return, when distress can take place immediately after the written demand. If the person then neglects or refuses to pay and at least £200 is still due, a distraint warrant will be issued either to a Customs collector or private, bailiffs. Warrants will also be delayed where any time to seek a review or appeal is unexpired. Where there is evidence to dispute all or a large part of an assessment, a review or appeal should be sought promptly.

- *local taxes and child support maintenance:* a liability order will precede the threat of bailiffs. The person should have received a copy of the order from the court and will therefore know how much is due including the court costs. Whether further steps are taken before bailiffs call is then largely at the discretion of the creditor. It is not possible to set aside the court order once made, so the only option is to negotiate with the local authority or CSA.

- *income tax*: the collector will send the tax payer demands for payment before taking further steps. These will be in writing and will be sent to the person's last known address. Normally the first demand will be issued by one of the central 'accounts offices' within a few days of payment being missed.

A couple of further demands will follow before the matter is passed to the local collector. The Collector will usually accept instalments, if only over a few months. The demands will specify the sums due, require payment within seven days and warn of the fact that default interest is accruing. If the tax is still unpaid, there will still be a further delay to give the person a 'reasonable' opportunity to pay and to give the Revenue a firm basis for inferring that the person is refusing or neglecting to pay. Thus immediate distress is wrongful.

- *rent-* There may be no warning of rent distress. The right of a landlord to distrain exists automatically when property is let. It need not be expressly mentioned in the tenancy agreement or lease although the right to distrain may be excluded by that agreement. The tenant has until the last minute of the day fixed for payments to pay and distress cannot be levied until the next day. Then, however the landlord may distrain immediately for all or part of the arrears. If the rent is due on a Sunday, the landlord can distrain on a Monday. The landlord need not demand the rent before distraining unless this is stipulated in the tenancy agreement.

- *judgments*: The judgment itself will have been preceded by a claim form. Notice of the judgment will also be received. A civil court judgment is payable by instalments. If an instalment is missed, in the High Court the judgment creditor may apply for a warrant for the whole debt to be issued to the sheriff's officer. In the county court a warrant cannot be issued until the debtor has defaulted on at least one instalment and so long as no previous execution is outstanding. The warrant then issued can be for a part of the debt or the whole outstanding balance.

- Part warrants may be issued for £50 or one monthly or four weekly instalments, whichever is the greater. When a warrant is issued the bailiff will, in either case, give some prior warning to the debtor.

- *fines:* as above the defendant should know of the prosecution and conviction and is likely to have been required to pay by instalments.

Time of the levy

Bailiffs levying execution and statutory distraint may distrain at any time of day. However this may be restricted by the code of practice under which the bailiff operates - for instance the CSA code acknowledges that distraint may be levied at any time but restricts levies to between 7am and 9pm unless the circumstances are exceptional. In levies for fines and road traffic penalties where the car is often the asset seized, visits will usually be at night as it is then that the vehicle is most likely to be at the house.

There are two exceptions to the above general rule. One is for VAT where the regulations only permit distress between 8am and 8pm, though, once started, a levy can continue outside these times. If the business liable for VAT trades partly or wholly outside these times, distress may be made at a convenient hour of opening. The other exception to this rule is in distress for rent where a levy should not occur between sunset and sunrise. If the bailiff levies distress for rent at the wrong hour the distress is 'illegal'.

Distress for rent should not be levied on Sundays or on public holidays like Christmas and Easter. One may assume that similar limitations will apply in statutory distraint. Execution may be levied on any day except on a Sunday, though it may occur on Sundays with permission of court in an emergency. Failing to comply with these restrictions will, as above, render the distress illegal.

Place of levy

The basic rule is that the debtor's goods may be seized *wherever* they are, normally from premises belonging to the debtor. This could include goods of the debtor found on the highway. Although bailiffs executing statutory distress may go anywhere in England and Wales, certain limits are placed on other bailiffs' movements:

- *in execution* the sheriff's officer is limited to his 'bailiwick' (i.e. county) and the county court bailiff may only operate within that particular court's area.

- *in distress for rent* the bailiff or landlord can only call at the rented premises unless goods have been fraudulently removed elsewhere or the tenant agrees to a levy elsewhere. The landlord may *not* levy off the premises in the street. There is an exception to this where goods are located in the street immediately outside the rented premises.

- *taxes*: Whilst there is no statutory limitation on premises at which distraint may be levied and the warrant permits the bailiff enter *any* house or premises during the daytime in order to levy distress, usually bailiffs are only directed by the tax collectors to business premises as there are most likely to be assets there.

Rights of entry

The basic rule applying to all bailiffs is that there is a right of entry which may be exercised without the use of force. If entry is forced or is otherwise improper, it will make the whole levy illegal and the debtor will need to consider the remedies described further in this book A criminal offence may also be committed. An unlawful entry is not only one gained by force but one gained by improper means, whether that describes the physical means of access or the circumstances surrounding the entry.

Unlawful entry also includes entry against the debtor's will. As a result if a person opens their door to a bailiff but refuses to allow them in, the bailiff would have no right to insist or to prevent the door being closed. The same applies if a person sees a bailiff about to enter their property, such as coming through a gate or up a path.

- *debtor's homes* are protected from any forced entry. This protection extends to all buildings within the boundary of the premises, i.e. sheds, garages etc.

- *separate, non-domestic premises*: private bailiffs levying distress can never break into any premises but there is an exception for execution- see later.

- *flats, maisonettes and bedsits*: The front door of a flat or bedsit cannot be forced. Thus peaceable entry of the main door of the building still means that the bailiff has yet to effect peaceable entry of the person's own door.

How may bailiffs exercise these basic rights of peaceable entry?

- *doors*: the bailiff may enter an open door or open an unlocked door. Breaking open a door or gate is trespass. Use of a locksmith to open a door is illegal. If the door is secured shut, it is illegal to force it open, but reasonable force may be used to see if a door is fastened.

- *windows*: a bailiff may climb through an open window or skylight and open one wider if necessary. A windowpane cannot be broken. Though a bailiff may open a closed but unfastened door he cannot open a closed but un-fastened window. The bailiff cannot open a closed, latched window and the fastening securing a window may not be removed.

- *walls*: the bailiff may climb over a wall or fence or walk across a garden or yard provided these are not damaged in the process. If the door, windows or wall, are already broken open, it would seem that the bailiff may enter.

- *keys*: Use of a landlord's pass key is illegal. It would not matter whether the bailiff found the key or it was provided by a landlord. If a key is left in the lock it seems it may be permissible to turn it like a door handle to open the door.

- *internal doors*: The bailiff may break open any door or cupboard both to find goods or to escape if he is locked in. No demand need be made before forcing each inner door, but this precludes unnecessary use of force.

Lawful uses of force: It is legal to use force to gain entry in a only a few very limited situations. If force is employed, when departing from a property the bailiff should leave it in a secure condition, and could be sued for any losses arising from a failure to do this.

- *income taxes* - the HMRC collector of taxes may force entry, though some demand for entry should be made first. Use of this power is very rare. The procedure for forcing entry is as follows. The collector must apply to a JP for a warrant which will be granted if the JP is satisfied there is a reasonable ground for believing the person is "neglecting or refusing" to pay.

Once issued the collector may only force entry under the warrant during the 'daytime'. The courts have decided that the collector ca*nnot* break in without a policeman/woman being present, presumably to prevent a breach of the peace

- *re-entry* - the bailiff may, following a valid seizure force entry on returning to a property. Typically the seizure will have been completed by the taking of walking possession. If the agreed payments cease, or negotiations over payment break down, the bailiff will return to remove the goods seized in order to sell them. Force may only be used to re-enter the property if he is being deliberately excluded. To show this he will have had to warn the debtor of the planned return so that failure or refusal to permit entry can be interpreted as intentional, thus justifying the use of force. Entry may also be forced after forcible ejection. However in this latter instance the bailiff must have made a full entry initially, not just a foot in the door. County court bailiffs require the permission of a district judge, even an indemnity from the claimant, before forced entry may be made.

- *separate or non-domestic premises* (e.g. a workshop or warehouse) may be entered forcibly but only in execution. This right does not apply if the non-domestic premises are connected to a dwelling, even though they may have separate entrances and no communicating doors- for instance a flat over a shop. The bailiff should make enquiry as to the presence of goods first, otherwise they risk trespassing.

- *stranger's premises* may be entered forcibly by a landlord with a police officer if an oath has been sworn before magistrates to the effect that there are grounds for believing goods have been fraudulently removed there. The sheriff may also break into a third party's house if goods have been taken there to avoid execution. Demand for entry should be made first. Also a bailiff may enter such premises peaceably to search for goods but will be a trespasser if either no goods are found or if inner doors are forced in the process.

Police presence A common threat is that of the police being called to attend at the bailiff's entry. A police officer may be asked to attend either before or during a levy or forced entry if a threat of violence can be shown to be anticipated or one occurs.

Police powers The police may enter any property if necessary in the course of their duty to prevent breaches of the peace, though they will need to show any entry was reasonably necessary in the circumstances. They can arrest the person who commits, or who they reasonably believe will commit, a breach of the peace.

The involvement of the police can only be justified by the bailiff if it can be shown that it was necessary because of the use of or threats of resistance or violence, or similar circumstances met on a previous visit.

Resisting entry If a wrongful entry is discovered it is permissible for the debtor to resist it- within limits. However, ejecting a bailiff who has entered legally can lead to forced re-entry and to the commission of an offence. The courts have sanctioned the use of reasonable force by the debtor to resist entry by bailiffs in three different contexts: where the bailiff's status was not disclosed; where the bailiff forces entry, and where the bailiff ignores a request not to enter. However there is a considerable problem with the use of self-help to resist illegal entry.

Failed entry If entry can't be gained at all the bailiff is unlikely to give up on the first visit. Notice of their attendance will be left (for instance HMRC leave a standard signed notice on VAT form 879) and further visits will be made at different times on different days. Discrete enquiries may also be made from neighbours as to person's presence or movements.

Showing identification

The bailiff should be carrying with him the warrant from the creditor which gives him the authority to call and seize goods. A person is entitled to know by what right the bailiff is acting, so the warrant should generally be produced for a person's examination automatically on calling at the property. In distress for rent, magistrates courts, road traffic penalties, local taxes and child support maintenance production of some document required by statute when the bailiff attends at the debtor's home. In the latter two cases the levy will be by private bailiffs who should carry written authorisation of the creditor, which should be shown to the debtor on request.

Detailed rules apply to magistrate's court bailiffs. Each bailiff is issued with an identity card bearing their photograph and a copy of the authorisation from the court, and this should be carried at all times and produced to the defendant when executing warrants. Bailiffs enforcing a warrant should show it to the defendant if it is in their possession, otherwise they should state where it is and what arrangements may be made to inspect it. Bailiffs are however entitled to enforce a warrant without having it in their possession. The warrant will be in the bailiff's possession if it is either on his person or in a nearby vehicle, but it is not acceptable if it is at an office locally. Sheriff's officers will show their 'warrant card' (their official identification bearing their photograph and name) on entry. The Collector of Taxes has sole responsibility for carrying out a distraint for income taxes but is normally accompanied by a bailiff to advise on the value of goods or act as an independent witness in the event of an alleged irregularity or complaint. The collector will carry a 'Collectors' Warrant' which provides proof of identity if required. The bailiff is required by HMRC to hold a general certificate or a sheriff's officer's identity card.

In distress for rent either the landlord or a certificated bailiff may distrain. Unless the landlord is a corporate body, he/she may distrain in person. In the latter case, and most often otherwise, a private bailiff, who must be certificated, will be used. If the landlord is a company, a director must hold a certificate to be able to distrain. Distress without a certificate is trespass. The bailiff must produce a certificate and warrant to the tenant or any other person present who appears to be in control of the premises. The county court certificate for rent, local taxes and road traffic penalties should only be shown when levying for such debts.

Under the NSEA it is required that in all situations agents should produce identification on request, such as a badge or identity card, together with a written authorisation to act on behalf of the creditor. All correspondence and documentation must be clear and unambiguous. Additionally agents should provide prompt information to debtors and in particular they should clearly explain (and provide notice in writing) the consequences of the seizure of their goods and specifically give details of the charges that could be incurred.

In addition in the NSEA stress is laid upon the need to respect the confidentiality of the debtor. If the bailiff finds that the only person present is, or appears to be, under the age of 18 the enforcement agents must depart, though they may ask when the debtor will be home If the only persons present are children who appear to be under the age of 12 enforcement agents must simply leave without making any enquiries. It is required that bailiffs should, so far as practical, avoid disclosing the purpose of their visit to anyone other than the debtor. Where the debtor is not seen, the relevant documents must be left at the address in a sealed envelope addressed to him/her.

Repeat levies

The general rule is that a second distress cannot be made for the same debt. Two separate situations are covered by this. A bailiff can't distrain again for the same debt after a completed levy.

Illegal second levies The bailiff cannot distrain again under a warrant if:

- *it is for the same debt* after a complete levy (there is now no debt due);
- *if he has levied for too little* previously (this is only distress for rent);
- *if the bailiff has abandoned goods*
- *if goods levied upon have been wholly lost* through negligence on the part of the bailiff;

Legal second levies A second levy on a warrant **is** permissible where:

- *there were insufficient goods* on a first visit to levy execution, as warrants of execution remain in force until the whole sum due has been collected. The bailiffs may make a partial levy but are entitled to wait until the levy can be completed rather than notify the claimant that there are no seizable goods;
- *the bailiff made a reasonable mistake* because of the uncertain value of the items;
- *circumstances at the auction* prevented the best price being obtained.
- *the debtor obstructed or attacked the bailiff* or refused entry;
- *the first distress was trespass*
- *the first distress is withdrawn* at the request of the debtor because instalments are agreed. If the arranged payments are not made, the bailiff can distrain again.

4

Seizure of Goods

Seizure

The act of seizure of the debtor's goods will involve a process of selecting and identifying items. There are two forms of seizure, described below:

- *actual seizure*: this will involve the bailiff actually seeing, even touching, the goods that are to be seized and listed for sale. It may well be coupled with a clear declaration of the bailiff's intention.

- *Constructive seizure:* this form of seizure is harder to define. The bailiff's intentions may be inferred from his actions, e.g. looking through a window, walking round premises, making and presenting a written notice of seizure and inventory of the goods being seized or by some means preventing the removal of certain goods. Physical contact is not essential provided that something has been done to intimate seizure has been made. The bailiff can seize one item or part of the goods in the name of all.

A bailiff is not necessarily entitled to all the goods on the premises and has to select sufficient to cover the debt and costs whilst ensuring this is not excessive. This involves some process of selection before seizure and where this fails to happen it may be possible to challenge whether any levy has taken place. Even though a valid seizure may have occurred, it must be stressed that the levy process is not yet complete. Seizure gives the bailiff immediate control of the goods, but they must now be impounded for the seizure to have any effect on the debtor and for the bailiff to *retain* control.

Impounding

Impounding is essential in order to change the status of the seized goods. For the bailiff to have the power to return later, break into the premises, remove the goods on the inventory and sell them, he must acquire some legal control over them. This is done by impounding. Technically, when the goods are impounded they are said to be placed in the 'custody of the law' and interference with them by the debtor or any one else will be 'poundbreach'. There are four different forms of impounding, one of which must be followed:

- *Immediate Removal*: the bailiff takes away the selected goods at the end of the first visit to a storeroom. This method is rarely used because of the expense and trouble involved except against businesses.

- *Locking up in a room on the premises* is permissible in distress for rent only and is seldom done. It is not permissible for a bailiff levying *any* other form of distraint or execution to lock up goods in a room on the premises. It is also illegal for *any* bailiff to impound goods by locking up the entire premises, thus completely excluding the occupier. This is tantamount to eviction and there is no power to do this. The warrant licences the bailiff to seize goods, not to seize a property, and to endeavour to take exclusive possession of premises in this way is trespass.

- *Close possession*: a bailiff can be left guarding the goods as 'possession man'. However, the cost and staffing problems associated with close possession means that it is virtually never used.

- *Walking possession*: this is the form of possession or impounding taken almost exclusively nowadays. Walking possession is a process whereby the debtor agrees (usually in writing) that the goods will remain in his premises, subject to the bailiff's possession and right to return and remove them for sale and also subject to payment of a daily fee to the bailiff.

Whose signature? .
Any 'responsible' person on the premises, including the spouse, partner, employee or adult relative of the debtor, can in most cases make the agreement. The debtor's authority or consent is not necessary and "responsible" has been defined as knowing the goods shouldn't be moved by anyone else, stopping them being removed and telling the bailiff if they are.

Children will not be able to make such agreements, nor, it is likely, will individuals only temporarily present in the property at the time the bailiff calls.

In local tax legislation much stricter requirements are laid down. The only acceptable signatory is the debtor named on the liability order, and he must sign at the time of the levy. If the debtor does not sign, no charges may be made

The courts have suggested that there are two forms of walking possession:

- *by agreement*: normally this will be the form encountered.

The bailiff will be keen to get a signed agreement with the debtor so that his position is clarified and so that he may add on charges for the possession.

- *by implication*: walking possession without any written agreement may be implied to arise in situations where the debtor acknowledges, or at least cannot deny, that seizure has occurred and that the bailiff has laid claim to certain goods. This can be described as a form of walking possession, as the circumstances will be the same in that the bailiff is absent from the property, leaving the goods with the debtor.
-

Clamping is frequently used by bailiffs of seizing/ impounding motor vehicles. This may be as a form of possession or as an interim means of immobilising a vehicle prior to the imminent arrival of a tow truck. there is nothing at present to indicate that the use of wheel clamps by bailiffs is legal, though its convenience is understandable. Clamping is therefore very likely to be trespass to the debtor's goods, and accordingly illegal.

Failed levies & abandonment

As already stated, for a valid levy to have been made both seizure and impounding must occur. There are a number of ways in which bailiffs can fail to follow the correct procedures outlined above.

Failed levies The common mistakes in taking possession seem to be as follows:

- *wrong place & time*: A possession agreement must be made at the correct stage in the levy process and in the correct circumstances in order to be valid. Thus the following agreements will be vulnerable to challenge by the debtor as there will have been no levy:

- *those posted to the debtor*- an 'agreement' must by definition be between two parties, and should be made at the time of seizure. A partially completed 'walking possession' agreement posted to the debtor cannot logically be of any validity as no document signed by one party alone - the bailiff - can constitute an agreement binding on the another, nor has there been any entry to the premises. Even if he subsequently signs and returns it, as is commonly requested, he is not waiving any fault with it or accepting the agreement. Signing the agreement retrospectively will not bar the debtor from any subsequent objection to its legality as one cannot, by one's actions, be deprived of one's rights in ignorance of what they are.

A valid walking possession agreement must follow a legal entry and levy and that paperwork dropped through the door for signature and return by the debtor is unacceptable and ineffective. The debtor may thus continue to deal with goods as he wishes as they are not in the custody of the law and cannot be until the bailiff has at least entered the property. Equally no walking possession fee may be charged.

- *those made at the office*- 'walking possession agreements' signed at the bailiff's office without entry or even visits to premises are, for the same reasons as above, void.

- *local tax & child support* agreements must be made at the time that distress is levied. If this is not done, there is no valid agreement as defined by the law, even if the bailiff comes back later and gets the debtor's signature.

- *wrong signature:* In most forms of distraint and execution any 'responsible person' may sign. For local taxes *only* the signature of the person named on the liability order will be acceptable. The signature of a spouse or partner will not do as a substitute. Because of the difficulty of always getting the liable person's signature, bailiffs often get someone else to sign. If the correct person cannot or will not sign, no walking possession fee may be charged. However the goods are probably still impounded by walking possession without agreement and the 'agreement' with the 'third party' is evidence of the bailiff's intention.

- *no written agreement*: If it is not possible to persuade the person to sign the bailiff may still manage to impound the goods by an oral agreement. Charges cannot be made and the bailiff's rights will be quite short lived. If steps are not taken to keep the possession in existence, e.g. follow up visits, letters or phone calls, or of course prompt removal, within a relatively short time the bailiff's rights will be lost. The goods are then 'abandoned' (see later) and the seizure process will have to be commenced again from the start.

- *wrong wording*: The wording used on the walking possession agreement is crucial. Several of the regulations also provide a standard form of agreement that bailiffs should use which the bailiff should follow closely. This is because of the differing phraseology used in the legislation.

  \- *distress for rent*: the standard form provided for use in rent distress states that walking possession is "*in consideration of [the bailiff] not leaving a man in close possession*".

  \- *distraint for local taxes & child support*. The regulations state that walking possession is "*in consideration of the [bailiff] not immediately removing the goods*". Some bailiffs firms use the standard distress for rent possession agreement in all contexts. The problem with this is that as the local tax and child support regulations state that the purpose of walking possession is something quite different from that in rent distress, the agreement is likely to be void. No charges may be made and no removal could follow from it. All the bailiff can do is reword the form and start the levy again.

- *no agreement:* If no agreement is made at all, either written or oral, the bailiff can leave notice on the premises that seizure has occurred and this will operate as a sort of walking possession to adequately impound the goods for a brief period. The notice and the debtor's presence during the seizure will be enough for the bailiff to have asserted his legal rights and for the debtor to understand what was intended. However, as described earlier, the right to force re-entry and remove will be transitory and soon lost unless the levy is quickly followed up. Of course, no charges can be made for possession in this situation. HMRC policy is that if it is not possible to get walking possession or to remove the goods immediately, the levy may be abandoned (see below).

- *Abandonment.* If the bailiff fails to maintain possession of the goods, they are then regarded as having been 'abandoned', i.e. by failing to remain adequately in possession or by delaying his return the bailiff loses any right to return and remove them. Essentially, whether goods have been abandoned depends on the individual facts of that case, and depends on the court deciding whether there has first been impounding and secondly whether there has been an intention to remain in possession.

Other aspects of levies & prior claims

The debtor does not have to be at the property for the bailiff to be entitled to enter and seize goods, though in the case of local taxes the debtor's signature is likely to be needed on documentation so in practice they will have to be there. HMRC policy is that if entry is gained but a 'person in authority' (i.e. a director, owner or partner) can't be found notice is left but the levy is not proceeded with. Sometimes other conditions are imposed on the levying bailiff by the creditor. For instance, the CSA code of practice requires that levies should only be carried out if the debtor is present.

Priority claims Another factor for the bailiff to take into account during a levy is prior claims to which the debtor is liable There may be little to be gained by the debtor raising such issues other than to disrupt the levy. However it may be that the bailiff abandons a levy rather than have to deal with the prior claimants. The main ones are the Crown and by landlords seeking rent arrears.

- *Crown priority* It is along established principle that the Crown is entitled to priority in recovery proceedings, whether it is enforcing by execution or by distress. If the Crown seeks to levy and finds a landlord or other creditor already in possession, it may proceed as its debt takes precedence providing the goods have not been sold. This cannot occur if the goods seized under the earlier levy have been sold, for then the goods are no longer the debtor's. The other likely Crown creditor to be encountered in this context is HMRC collecting VAT. If the Department exercises their right to distrain, a later levy will attain priority over any earlier bailiff. If such debts exist it might be worthwhile drawing them to the bailiff's attention as he might withdraw if there is a risk his claim to the goods will be overridden.

- *Landlord's claims* Landlords are given priority rights in execution and distress for road traffic penalties only to claim payment for arrears of rent due under a current tenancy. These rights do not apply to other forms of distress, such as for local taxes.

  The bailiff is under no liability to enquire as to the existence of rent arrears, but if notice of a claim is received (for instance from the tenant) the bailiff should investigate it. When a claim is received the county court or road traffic bailiff should then levy for the rent and costs. Upon sale the bailiff will satisfy firstly the costs of the sale, then the landlord's claim not exceeding:

  - four weeks' rent where the rent is due weekly; or,

  - two month's rent where the rent is due monthly; and (of course),

  - the sum for which the warrant was issued.

  A similar procedure is followed by the sheriff's officer. Again, the only benefit of such rights to the debtor may be that they persuade the bailiff to withdraw rather than incur further costs in what might be an unproductive levy.

What can be seized

Bailiffs can normally seize both the debtor's goods and money (including banknotes and cheques). Only enough to cover the debt and costs can be seized. The NSEA requires that bailiffs should take all reasonable steps to satisfy themselves that the value of the goods impounded is proportional to the value of the debt and charges due. Further, a large number of categories of item are exempt, as will be described in the following sections. If any exempt goods are seized, there may be two implications for the bailiff:

- If *only* exempt goods have been seized, the whole levy will be illegal and will be trespass.
- If some exempt goods have been seized along with items that might lawfully be taken, the levy is only trespass and unlawful as far as the exempt property is concerned and any claim for damages would be limited to those items alone. The whole levy would not be invalidated.

The onus of proof is on the debtor to show that the goods seized are exempt because they fall in any particular category or below any financial limit. However bailiffs have a duty of care that they must exercise when seizing goods. They must act with discernment and judgment. If, during an actual levy, the bailiffs are put on notice that certain goods do not allegedly belong to the debtor, they must act with due caution and circumspection and try to seize other items if possible. If they do not, an illegal levy may have occurred. The categories of seizable and exempt goods are as follows. Distress for rent is dealt with separately because of its unique nature. If any of these rules are breached, an action for wrongful interference or replevin may be possible.

Valuable goods

The bailiff can only seize property that can be sold. As a consequence items that cannot be sold such as deeds, personal papers or effects should not be the subject of a levy. Items of no or minimal value should also not be seized (e.g. old or broken possessions).

Only those goods belonging to the debtor may be taken. This does however mean that jointly owned goods may be seized, though the proceeds must be divided between the owners according to their shares. Most regulations for statutory distraint refer to the "goods of the debtor" so that it is possible that jointly owned goods cannot be seized in such cases. In child support maintenance distress it is provided that the goods needed to satisfy the basic domestic needs of the debtor include those needed by any member of the family with whom s/he resides. This unique provision presumably is intended to protect any new spouse and children the liable person may have. HMRC has voluntarily decided not to seize joint goods.

Utility fittings & fixtures
Fixtures that are actually attached (e.g. ranges/ovens) cannot be taken as they are part of the property, not goods and chattels.

Finally there are specific exemptions from seizure for pipes, meters and cables belonging to utilities.

Goods subject to prior levies
Those items already seized in execution or distress cannot normally be seized again, for instance goods seized in distress for rent cannot be seized in execution. There is an exception to this general rule for the Crown.

Third parties' goods
Assets belonging to lodgers, relatives and other third parties may not be seized. There are exceptions to this general rule in distress for rent. If such items are taken, the person generally has a remedy - such as interpleader or an action for wrongful interference in the county court. A third party may prove ownership by seeking to make in prescribed form a statutory declaration of their position- a sworn confirmation of ownership made before a JP, court officer or solicitor, which could be presented to the bailiff in an effort to avoid the necessity of court proceedings.

Children's goods

Children can deal with property in the same manner as adults i.e. purchase, own and dispose of goods in the normal fashion. Thus, where property is given to a child, it becomes the child's as soon as the gift is made. In consequence items bought by children, or for children, and presents to them, ought not to be seized by bailiffs. The NSEA states that when seizing goods bailiffs should not remove anything clearly identifiable as an item belonging to, or for the exclusive use of, a child.

Spouses' and partners' goods

Bailiffs may seek to seize the property of one spouse to satisfy the debts of the other. The existing case law relates to the rights of a married woman, but the general principles will apply to cohabitees as well. The following relates to wives, but may of course be reversed to apply to husbands facing enforcement against their goods for their wives' debts.

A married woman may purchase, own, sell and give away any property in all respects as if she is a single person. All property belonging to woman at marriage or acquired by or devolving upon her after that date belongs to her as if she is single. If the items are bought by the husband for the wife's own personal use (e.g. for birthdays, anniversaries or Christmas), they will be gifts.

Problems can arise in respect of items bought by the couple after marriage. The courts generally assume an intention to share any property acquired, and divide it up equally. Housekeeping money or property acquired with that will be treated as shared equally unless it is clearly intended to be shared otherwise. Where there is a joint bank account or other common pool of income, the wages of one spouse are generally seen as being earned on behalf of both. Items bought from such an account therefore would be regarded as jointly owned and seizable. This is not the case where one spouse provides all the income in a joint account, which is simply used as a matter of administrative convenience. The money (and thus the acquisitions) belong to the person providing it.

If third party goods are seized, the owner may sue or replevy (see later). In cases of execution *interpleader* may also be an available remedy.

Interpleader applies to sheriffs officers, county court bailiffs and those enforcing road traffic debts. It is a process by which the creditor and a third party make claims against one another (interplead) so that the ownership of the property may be decided by the court. It may also be used by the bailiff to gain protection against other court actions arising out of any substantial grievance caused by his wrongful acts. Claims to property seized from the debtor may be made by a wide range of individuals- for example, partners, spouses, relatives, friends, lodgers, trade suppliers, trustees in bankruptcies and hire or HP firms.

The procedure is as follows:

- *Notice* - In all cases, the claimant should put their claim in writing. In the High Court the third party must give notice of the claim, including a full description of goods, to the sheriff, who must forthwith notify the execution creditor, sending a copy of the claim. The creditor must then, within seven days, give notice whether or not the claim is admitted or disputed. If the creditor admits the claim, the sheriff withdraws. If the creditor disputes the claim or fails to reply, the sheriff can apply to the Court for protection against any proceedings relating to the seizure and should withdraw from possession of the goods claimed. Protection from being sued by the owner will normally be granted but will not be where there is a substantial grievance against the bailiff which seems serious enough to override this immunity.

In the county court the claimant serves notice on a county court District Judge if the levying bailiff will not accept his/her claim. The district judge then notifies the creditor and requires a reply in four days. If notice is received within four days admitting the claim the bailiff is withdrawn. The District Judge may then seek an order from the Circuit Judge restraining any action being brought by the third party as a result of the disputed seizure. Normally the District Judge will be protected but, as with the sheriff, this may be overridden.

- *Application* - In the High Court, if the claim is disputed by the execution creditor the sheriff applies for 'interpleader' and notifies the creditor and claimant. Within fourteen days, the claimant must serve on the other parties an affidavit specifying goods and chattels claimed and the grounds for the claim. In the county court if no reply is received or the creditor refuses to return of the goods then an interpleader claim form is issued on N88 to the parties and a hearing of the case is arranged.

- *Security deposit*- the High Court may order payment of a deposit or the provision of security. and the county court must require this when accepting any interpleader claim against its own bailiff. This requirement does not apply to interpleader against road traffic bailiffs. The security may be a solicitor's undertaking, a bond from a bank or insurance company or a guarantee from a person with two other sureties. The purpose of the deposit is to place in the court's control a sum equivalent to the value of the disputed goods and, if the claimant wishes the bailiff to withdraw, a sum representing the costs that the bailiff has incurred up until that date. This fund then becomes the subject matter of the dispute and the goods are released to the claimant and cannot be seized again by that creditor. In the county court if no deposit is paid the goods must be sold and the proceeds paid into court to await the judge's decision unless the judge decides otherwise in the circumstances. If less than the value is deposited the bailiffs must not withdraw and the court can order the bailiff to retake possession.

- *Sale of goods*: the court may order sale of the goods and that the proceeds be paid out as it orders. This may be done where:

  - the goods are perishable;

  - the safety of the goods is uncertain, for instance because the debtor won't agree to walking possession; or,

  - the claimant fails to provide the security required by the court.

- *Damages*: in county court cases the claimant may claim any damages he/she feels were incurred within 8 days of receiving the claim form. In the High Court any such claim must be made in a separate case. If it is proved that there is a 'substantial grievance' or that substantial injury has been suffered, damages should be awarded. The kind of factors taken into account by the court when considering an award of damages will include:

- where the bailiff has entered the premises of a stranger and seized that person's goods; or

- where the claim arose from the bailiff's own wrongful actions- for instance, there has been an assault, goods were seized in the knowledge that they were not the debtor's or that they were already seized in distress.

- *Hearing* - The High Court can decide the case in a summary way if all parties consent or one so requests or if the dispute is about interpreting the law, rather than the facts, and the case is straightforward. If there appears to be a dispute as to ownership between the claimant and debtor, the court may order a trial in the High Court or county court. If the claimant fails to attend or fails to comply with the order made, the Court may bar him/ her from any future claims. If the execution creditor doesn't appear the sheriff is ordered to withdraw from possession. The sheriff will of course be told to withdraw if the third party's claim is established. If the claimant only establishes ownership of some of the goods, s/he is entitled to be paid from the deposit a sum representing the value of those goods, though the execution creditor will receive the balance. Similar orders may be made in the county court.

Statutory exemptions

Basic tools and household items are exempt from seizure in all but VAT and magistrates court distraint. The exemptions are:

- "such tools, books, vehicles and other items of equipment as are necessary for use personally in business ,employment or vocation". This exemption is not limited to tools only capable of being carried by the debtor. However if a tool is occasionally used by another, it is not protected. Note also that under business rates distraint the only goods protected are basic household items, **not** tools of the trade; and,

- "such clothing, bedding, furniture, household equipment and provisions as are necessary for satisfying the basic domestic needs of the person and family".

These exclusions are phrased very broadly. There have been various attempts to define what is meant. The Lord Chancellor's Department has provided guidance for county court bailiffs. For example it is suggested that:

- *tools* will only be protected if they are so essential that without them there is no way that the debtor's present business or job could continue;

- *motor vehicles* will only be treated as a necessity in exceptional cases. Either the vehicle will be needed to continue a job or business or to get to work, and there will be no reasonable alternative;

- *household necessities* are not likely to include stereos, televisions, videos and microwaves.

In the High Court if a dispute arises as to whether goods fall within the exempt categories, the sheriff may apply for instructions from the Court by using the interpleader process described earlier. The procedure is for the debtor to give written notice of the claim that the goods are exempt within five days of their seizure. The sheriff must then serve notice of this claim on the execution creditor, who has seven days to accept or dispute the exemption. If the creditor does not respond or admits that the items are exempt, the sheriff withdraws from possession. If the claim of exemption is disputed, the sheriff seeks a court. The Court will normally hear and determine the claims summarily. In the county court disputes are referred to a District Judge.

There are two exceptions to these general categories of exempt goods:

- *in magistrates court* the exempt household items are limited to beds and clothes of the person and family. The broad exemption of tools of the trade described above applies however. The term beds may be construed to include bedclothes as well as the bed frame.

- *VAT distress* has its own unique list of exempt goods that has recently been introduced. These are any of the following which are located in the home at which distraint is levied and which are reasonably required to meet the domestic needs of any person living there. The exempt goods are: beds and bedding; household linen; chairs and settees; tables; food; lights and light fittings; heating appliances; curtains; floor coverings; furniture, equipment and utensils used for cooking, storing and eating food; refrigerators; articles for cleaning, pressing and mending clothes; articles for cleaning the home; furniture used for the storing clothing, bedding or household linen; cleaning articles or utensils for cooking and eating food; articles used for safety in the home; toys for the use of any child in the household and medical aids and equipment. On business premises the exempt goods are limited to fire fighting equipment for use on those premises and medical aids and equipment for use there.

Motor vehicles

Motor vehicles may be seized like any other asset, and are often the most valuable and easily accessible of the debtor's possessions. There is almost no legal guidance as to the procedure to be followed in seizing vehicles but it would appear that the same rules of location and entry apply as in any other levy situated. Whilst the vehicle itself may be levied upon, there is no reason to suppose that items within it may be taken if that involves forced entry and any such entry is likely to be illegal. Impounding should be by notice, walking possession or removal as already described, but clamping is frequently used.

Before removal a bailiff will normally check ownership with Hire Purchase Information and DVLA. If the results of this are satisfactory it is normal to remove promptly. When doing this any personal contents in the vehicle are usually either returned to the debtor or listed in the presence of a witness. If possible the registration documents and keys are obtained from the debtor or another responsible person. Normally removal is by towing or loading on transporter. Bailiffs should use reasonable care when arranging a contractor to move the vehicle, but, provided this is done, they are not liable generally for any negligence on the part of the contractor. If the car is damaged, the owner will have to sue the haulage firm, not the bailiffs.

Rent levies

Distress for rent is the exception to the previous statements because:

- the basic rule is that any item on the rented premises may be taken, regardless of ownership, but,
- this right has been modified by statute and some goods are

now exempted, or 'privileged', as the following paragraphs describe.

Readers should note that all the categories of exemption (or privilege) are separate exclusive clauses i.e. tools are protected even if they are not in use.

Qualified privilege
The items granted 'qualified' or conditional privilege can only be taken if there are insufficient other goods. The landlord may be sued for seizing goods with qualified privilege unless he genuinely believed that there were no alternative items. The privileged items comprise a number of items of little modern relevance but do include:

- *tools of the trade* in excess of those protected by absolute privilege (see below).

Absolute privilege
Items given absolute privilege are exempted completely from seizure. They include:

- *perishable items* and *loose money* (i.e. not in a purse or wallet);

- *things in actual use* including clothes being worn;

- *household goods and tools of the trade* as protected in the county court. Tools of the trade can include items hired or on HP in a spouse's name so that he can earn a living for the whole family e.g. a sewing machine;

- *goods held in the course of business* on trade premises as a direct part of the tenant's business. The trade must be 'public' i.e.

anyone can approach the trader to use his services. The exemption covers all goods "carried, wrought or managed in the way of trade or employ". There is no need for the goods to be altered whilst in the trader's hands. The privilege will cover items left for repair, furniture held in store, goods on pawn or at an auctioneer's and goods held by a sale agent acting on commission.

- *goods on hire purchase or conditional sale* subject to a default notice, a suspended delivery order or a termination notice. This is a strange situation where it is actually advantageous to be in debt. Also if the goods are subject to an agreement in the tenant's spouse's name, they are protected, but not if they are in joint names.

- *hired and leased goods:* A recent decision held that goods hired or leased can no longer be regarded as the tenant's property and were thus now exempt from distress for rent.

- *third party's goods:* The property of lodgers, sub-tenants, strangers and other unconnected third parties is absolutely privileged. If it is seized by mistake these individuals must make a written declaration to the landlord in a set form accompanied by an inventory stating that items levied upon are theirs. Such declarations can only be made within a reasonable time after distress. Sub-tenants must also undertake to pay any rent direct to the landlord until the tenant's arrears are cleared. On receiving a declaration the landlord should return the goods and to continue to distrain would render it illegal. If this is not done the person may apply before two JPs for a restoration order. If any such third party goods are seized by the landlord the owner can be reimbursed for their value by the tenant owing the rent.

No privilege

No privilege is given to the goods of the following:

- *the tenant's spouse*;

- *a person who has lent goods* to the tenant. Goods on 'permanent loan' with no conditions attached would be seizable; or,

- *a business partner*: Application may be made by way of complaint by a claimant to magistrates court for a determination as to whether goods are covered by this subsection.

Notices & inventories

Having completed the seizure the bailiff will commonly leave at the property or with the debtor a notice of seizure confirming what has occurred. Notices will commonly include the following information-

- a *statement of the debt due and costs* incurred so far (including the statutory scale of charges);

- an *inventory* of the goods seized, and;

- often, a *walking possession agreement*. Though strictly speaking this is a separate document, it is often incorporated in to the notice of seizure for convenience.

The relevant legislation may require other information to be left, such as a copy of the relevant regulations and notice of any rights to appeal, interplead or replevy, plus details of the bailiff's certificate, if it is a rent, local tax or road traffic levy. Where a notice must be left, failure to provide one, or provision of an inadequate notice, will make the distress irregular. No notice at all is required from the HMRC but the practice of the latter is to require that notice of distraint plus an inventory are be left on VAT form 825, attached to which will be any walking possession agreement made, on form 824.

Certain errors on notices will **not** invalidate them- in the name of the debtor, in the date the debt fell due or in not including the date at all. A notice does not have to be presented personally to the debtor in distress for rent or local taxes. No inventory need be given in distress for income tax, VAT or local taxes- in other cases this information must be provided. The CSA code requires that all items seized should be listed in duplicate on an inventory attached to the walking possession agreement. All reasonable steps should be taken to verify ownership and an estimated sale value should be endorsed on the inventory. The collector must always give a written notice of distraint including a detailed inventory of the goods concerned.

Magistrates court bailiffs have a statutory duty to state the reasons for the issue of the warrant that has been executed. It is also provided that the contract between the MCC and the enforcement agency should require the bailiff to hand to the defendant a leaflet providing the following information:

- the purpose of the visit by the bailiff;
- the powers vested in the enforcement agency;
- how any sum due, in respect of which the warrant being executed was issued, may be paid;
- where advice about the effect of the warrant and related matters may be obtained;
- the charges that may be made in respect of the warrant;
- details of the complaints procedures operated by the MCC and the agency.

Form of inventories Case law has established that where an inventory is supplied, it must make it clear what goods have been seized. A notice should either:

- list and identify each item seized, or
- imply that all goods on the premises have been seized. The courts have said that this is permissible, if unsatisfactory.

See Appendix 1 for sample interpleader claim.

5

Sales of Goods

Making payment

A large percentage of levies lead to instalments being arranged before anything is taken. This is the most sensible way of settling the matter.

Instalments

Bailiffs in the civil courts can be made to accept instalments and withdraw if the court consents to suspending the execution on terms. In other forms of distress there is no option for the debtor to make application to the court and s/he will have to rely on negotiation with the bailiff or creditor.

Difficulties may arise for both the debtor and the bailiff when an affordable payment cannot be agreed. This is usually because of the time scales for recovery laid down by creditors.

Rules on payment

There are some legal restrictions as to how payment may be made by the debtor, when it must be accepted by the bailiff or creditor and the impact thereof. Reference is often made in the regulations to 'tender' of payment of a debt and costs. Tender is an unconditional offer to pay the full sum of debt and costs, whether by means of cash, a banker's draft or a building society cheque. The money should be produced at the same time as making the offer. Tender may be made to the creditor or bailiff and either should accept. Offering a current account cheque or part payment by instalments does not qualify as valid tender, though the bailiff or creditor may accept such a method of settling a debt and may suspend enforcement until the cheque is cleared or instalments are completed, rather than withdrawing the levy altogether.

The right to tender payment is not continuous. There are stages in the enforcement process when costs are accruing and cannot be accurately calculated until the activity has ended- for example, during a removal. A person may in such cases only pay before the process begins, or after it has ceased when the amount due is clear, but not during the process.

If tender is made between seizure and impounding, it would be illegal for the bailiff to proceed to impound or remove. After seizure, but before removal, if the debt and costs are tendered any removal or retention of the seized goods is illegal but does not make either preceding act wrongful. After removal but before sale tender of the debt and costs renders any sale irregular, but not illegal, so that the debtor could only sue for any provable loss. Refusal of a valid tender also gives the tenant the right to rescue the goods or to make a court claim.

Effect of payment

If payment is properly made, the effect on the levy is laid out in the relevant regulations. For example:

- *Child support maintenance:* If the sums due are paid or tendered to the Secretary of State or bailiff before sale, the payment should be accepted and the distraint will not proceed, any sale being cancelled and the goods being made available for collection by the debtor.

- *local taxes:* If, after seizure, the outstanding balance of the tax, plus the costs of the magistrate's claim form and the bailiff's fees are paid or tendered, the billing authority must accept the amount and the goods cannot be sold. The debtor can then collect them.

- *rent:* The bailiff can receive payment and should not be told to refuse it by the landlord. If the distress were to be continued the tenant could apply to the county court for an injunction and an order to return the goods.

- *execution*: If payment or tender is made to the bailiff, he must withdraw from possession, the execution is discharged and sale may not take place.

- *road traffic penalties* If, after seizure but before sale of the goods, the debtor pays or tenders to the local authority or bailiff the debt due plus costs the levy is superseded and the goods must be released. It is also interesting to note that the levy may also be terminated by the council accepting a lesser sum in full satisfaction of the debt due- a concession unique to such forms of distress.

Removal

Removal will not usually happen until at least five days after seizure, not including the day of the levy. This timescale is set by statute for some bailiffs, but has been adopted as good practice by others. If goods are to be removed the bailiff will return to the debtor's premises where the goods have been impounded and if necessary may force entry to 'uplift' the goods. On return only what was previously seized may be removed. If extra goods are discovered after the seizure and notice was presented, they cannot be included in the levy and to remove them would be an illegal second levy.

In distress for rent and road traffic penalties certain procedural requirements apply at this stage. Firstly a detailed breakdown of the costs should be left by handing it to the person. This details the number of vehicles used, the number of men employed, the number and type of special removal machines, the time spent at the property and loading and unloading the vans and the basic charge for each item. Secondly in rent cases notice of where the goods are stored shall be given to the tenant or left at the house within one week of the deposit of those items (the week does not include the day of removal). If and when removal occurs, the goods should not be removed from the county in which they were seized. The landlord or bailiff may be subject to a penalty if this is wrongfully done.

Care should be taken by bailiff when removing and storing goods otherwise an action for negligence could be brought by the debtor. The NSEA states that when removing goods a receipt for items taken should be given to the debtor or left at the premises. Bailiffs must also ensure that goods are handled with reasonable care so that they do not suffer any damage whilst in their possession and should have insurance to cover goods in transit.

Public auctions

There will normally be a further delay of at least five days between seizure and sale of goods in order to allow for advertising and preparing the sale. Sales may occasionally take place earlier if the goods are perishable or the debtor consents in writing. The advantage of the delay is to give a person a further chance to pay the debt or make other arrangements to recover the goods seized.

The manner of sale varies according to the form of distress involved, though it is normally by public auction. The bailiff cannot hand goods over to the creditor but both the creditor and the debtor can buy them at the sale. Care should be taken to properly advertise any sale that occurs.

There is no requirement to set a reserve price before sale except for taxes (the Collector will have this done by an auctioneer or some other qualified person). In most cases the debtor can, at his her own expense, request that competent persons carry out an appraisement or valuation of the goods. If goods are sold for greatly under their value the debtor may have a substantial grievance upon which a claim for damages could be based. However the onus is on the claimant to show that there was substantial difference between the price realised and the value at the date of sale. The prices raised at auctions are notoriously low and while the auction price is not conclusive proof of the value of the goods it may be very difficult after the event for a person to come up with other proof of the value of their goods.

If the goods are of a specialist nature, it is the bailiff's duty to obtain advice on the mode of sale- for instance advertising in specialist press. A claim for damages can be issued for not selling at the best price, giving evidence of mismanagement in connection with the handling of the goods at the sale. Improper lotting and hurrying the sale has been held to invalidate it. A bailiff acts wrongfully by seizing and selling more than is "reasonably sufficient" to cover the debt and costs, though obviously there must be a margin for error and a reasonable amount may be seized in the first place. If several items, each worth more than the debt due, are seized and all are sold, this is trespass as no more than is necessary to pay the debt and costs should be sold. It is therefore the bailiff's duty to closely monitor a sale to make sure that too much is not sold.

Special rules on sales apply to the different forms of seizure:

- In the *High Court* if the debt and expenses exceed £20 the sale must be by public auction which should be advertised for at least three days beforehand but the sheriff should allow reasonable time before sale to allow claims for interpleader. The court can set aside a sale if the sheriff did not take reasonable care to advertise it, leading to a sale at undervalue. The sale can be on the debtor's premises with his/her consent. If no reasonable price can be obtained the claimant should be notified and the sheriff should await further instructions.

- In the county court, goods are held for five days before sale. The sale should be advertised for three days previously and is by public auction unless the court orders otherwise. The debtor must have four days' notice of the time and place of the auction. Private sale cannot be ordered where the debt is less than £20 but otherwise the court can order this on application from the creditor or debtor. Any other creditor enforcing against the debtor should be given four days notice of the hearing and can attend to make representations. Sale passes good title and creditors making claims against the debtor cannot recover any sums for the sale of the goods unless the court had notice of their claims or "reasonable enquiry" would have shown that the goods were not the judgment debtor's.

- For *rent*, although the landlord has the power to sell, s/he is under no obligation to do so. However after five days from, but not including, the date of the distress, if the arrears remain unpaid or replevin has not been commenced, he may sell for the best price that may be obtained. This period of five days can be extended to fifteen at the tenant's request, in order to allow replevin.

- For *local taxes* it is recommended that sale should generally occur after at least five days after seizure, although no minimum time period between seizure and sale is set in the regulations. Public auction is the usual method recommended but private treaty could be employed if the debtor consents.

- Road traffic penalties- the goods seized must be held at least five days before the sale. Only sale at public auction is possible. Claims by third parties to the goods will not prevent sale passing good title unless the claims are received before the sale or "reasonable enquiry" by the bailiff would have revealed them.

- VAT: Seized goods shall be kept for at least five days. Then, unless the tax due and the costs paid, the seized items shall be sold, though no mode or place of sale is specified in the legislation.

- Magistrates court rules set limits upon when the sale may occur. The goods cannot be sold earlier than six days after the levy unless a person gives written consent. Further if a period for sale is not specified on the warrant, sale should be no later than fourteen days after levy. The sale shall be by public auction unless the person consents in writing to some other method.

- Child support maintenance regulations set no minimum period before sale, though probably at least five days will generally be allowed.

Neither the Act or the regulations prescribe a method of sale though public auction is likely to be the rule. If goods are removed for sale the CSA code requires that the debtor must be informed by the bailiff of its date, time and location.

- Income tax: The collector must wait a minimum of five days before sale, which must be by public auction. Time is usually allowed to give the defaulter time in which to find the money or, in certain circumstances, to come to a suitable arrangement.

Accounts & proceeds

The proceeds should be paid over to the creditor promptly. The debtor is entitled to receive any surplus after paying the debt and costs and any goods that remain unsold. Any unsold goods will be returned to the place of seizure or left at a more convenient location, details of which will be notified to the tenant, for collection. The surplus may be held until the debtor claims it- there is no need to search for him. A landlord who sells enough to clear the debt should leave any surplus with the sheriff and return any surplus goods to where they were seized.

As soon as is practicable after completing the distraint, the magistrates court clerk must be sent a written account of costs and charges. The defaulter can inspect this within one month of the levy at a reasonable time to be set by the court .

6

The Bailiffs Costs

Costs

The costs chargeable by bailiffs are regulated by scales found in the statutes and statutory instruments that apply to each form of distress. Typical elements within these are:

- fixed fees for certain activities such as visits;
- 'reasonable' costs of removal and storage;
- fees for levies and auctions based on a percentage of the debt; and,
- VAT is included in the local tax and child support scale charges, but is additional to charges for distress for rent etc.

In the county court charges are simpler. For the issue of a warrant of execution a fee is paid upfront by the creditor. There are then no other charges unless and until a sale occurs.

The debtor is usually given a copy of the scale at the time of the levy. This can be used to check the bailiff's bill. With respect to fees the NSEA states that bailiffs must, on *every* occasion when a visit is made which incurs a fee for the debtor, leave a notice detailing both the charges made to date (including the one for that visit) and the fees which will be incurred if further action becomes necessary.

Magistrates courts In the magistrates court there is no statutory scale and each court will negotiate separately with its bailiffs. A bailiff can be fined for exacting high or improper costs but it is not possible for a defendant to seek detailed assessment of charges made in the levy of magistrate's distraint as there is no statutory provision providing a scale of charges.

Each charge scale will be individually negotiated with the relevant magistrates court, but will typically include elements to cover initial administrative costs on the issue of the warrant, attendance and levy charges and charges for removal- particularly of vehicles. Note that these costs are not added on to the sum if it remains unpaid and the matter returns to the court for committal proceedings. This because the penalty due only includes court costs and the court has no liability for any charges, even in cases where the levy is unsuccessful. Only the defaulter can be made to pay.

Recovery of costs

As a rule the bailiff's costs are included with the debt due and are recoverable as part of the total sum. Under income tax and local tax legislation it is specifically provided that where payment is made for less than the full sum due (including costs), it shall be applied to the costs first.

In all cases, if the debt is paid, without the costs, before any seizure has occurred the right to distrain ceases. If the debt is paid to the creditor and the bailiff is instructed to withdraw, the bailiff would not be able to proceed to recover any costs by sale. If the creditor instructs the bailiff to withdraw any authority to sell is lost as the bailiff is acting as the creditor's agent. If the creditor loses the right to enforce, the bailiff cannot sell goods for fees. The costs of previous unsuccessful levies should not be included in later levies as these are only payable out of proceeds of the first and may not be carried over to another: the debtor is under no personal liability for them

Bailiff's charges

Bailiffs can charge for activities not covered by the above scales, such as writing to the debtor prior to levy, setting up and administering an instalment payment scheme, writing to the debtor when an instalment scheme fails, or where a cheque bounces, making and receiving phone calls and negotiating with a client. Letters and negotiation are specifically allowed for in a few scales: for instance for sending a warning latter in road traffic enforcement or for negotiations between landlord and tenant in distress for rent.

Reasonable charges that are of direct benefit to the debtor may be permissible. Thus, if the charges simply reflect the cost to the bailiff of providing the facility and include no element of profit, and if they are demonstrably of assistance to the debtor and he had explicitly consented to them, they may be acceptable to the courts.

When considering whether a charge is lawful, certain principles should be borne in mind:

- *reasonability*: the court must consider if the sums billed are a fair charge for the work done. For example the court may reduce excessive van charges.

- *applicability*: the court can consider if the charges are being made at the correct stage in the process as envisaged by Parliament. An example might be the correct point for charging van fees. Arguably these should be charged when removal is threatened. Some firms charge for a vehicle sent when the levy took place, on the basis that although walking possession was agreed, it might have been necessary to remove. Some firms charge van fees even before they have levied, which is impossible to justify under the wording of the regulations.

- *illegality*: finally the court may conclude that the charges are totally unjustified by the scale.

Disputing a bill

There are a number of remedies.

Detailed assessment

Assessment is the process by which a court reviews a legal bill (whether from a solicitor or a bailiff) and approves or reduces the sum charged. Any of the scale costs are open to assessment by a county court. The notable exception from these powers is magistrates court distraint where the charges are set by the contract between bailiff and court, and are not laid down in regulations. Application is made by the debtor on a Part 8 claim form in the county court within three months of the receipt of the bill (see example). A hearing is arranged before a district judge at which the bill is examined. Any doubts as to reasonability shall be resolved in favour of the paying party. In assessing reasonability of charges regard may be had to the following factors:

- *the ratio between charges and sum due*: disproportionate charges will be disallowed;
- *the work involved*: if one levy is conducted for several warrants simultaneously, charges may be restricted to those allowable for one levy. The court will take into account the effort involved by the bailiff in preparation, travelling, attendance and follow up reports;
- *the period for which charges are made*: for example possession charges shouldn't be for unreasonable time without the debtor's consent.

The district judge may make such order for costs as s/he thinks fit, the debt being increased by such costs if awarded against the debtor.

Application for detailed assessment

In the County Court

No. Of Matter: **In the matter of:** the Local Government Finance Act 1992, and the Council Tax (Administration & Enforcement) Regulations 1992.

Between: *Applicant*

and

Respondent

Of applies to the court for an order in the following terms:-

1) Detailed assessment under CPR Part 47 of the bill of charges presented by in connection with a levy of distraint for council tax.
2) Directions as to costs as the court thinks fit.

The grounds on which the applicant claims to be entitled to the order are:-

1) The court has the power to conduct a detailed assessment of charges for distraint under para 3(2) Sch 5 Council Tax (Administration & Enforcement) Regulations 1992.
2) Charges for removal and storage, made under the scale found in para 1 Sch 1 of the above regulations, must be reasonable.
3) Following a levy of distraint on xth x 2008 under a liability order issued by Magistrates Court to London Borough of on 2008,

the defendants removed goods *(specify)* and submitted a bill showing a charge of £x for removal and storage. A copy of the bill is attached.
4) The applicant submits that these charges are unreasonable in the circumstances.

The names and addresses of the persons upon whom it is intended to serve this application are:-

Bailiffs

The claimant's address for service is:-

Dated this xth day of x 2008. Signed: Claimant

7

Rights of Redress

Making a complaint to the bailiff

The NSEA requires that enforcement agencies operate complaints and disciplinary procedures with which their staff must be fully conversant. The complaints procedure for debtors should be set out in plain English, have a single point of contact, set time limits for dealing with complaints and have an independent appeal process where appropriate. A register should be maintained to record all complaints. Enforcement agencies are encouraged to make use of the complaints and disciplinary procedures of professional associations such as the Association of Civil Enforcement Agencies or the Certificated Bailiffs' Association. There must also be an internal disciplinary procedure for members of staff within the enforcement agency. The enforcement agent must make available details of the complaints procedure on request by the debtor or when circumstances indicate it would be appropriate to do so.

For bailiffs enforcing fines for magistrate's courts, rules require that the firms operate internal complaints procedures. These should be publicised to debtors along with details of the court's own complaints scheme.

Complaining to the creditor

Any problem should be taken up initially with the bailiff's firm. If this is not successful one may turn to the creditor instructing them. One should also keep that organisation informed of any earlier negotiations by copying all correspondence to the relevant officer or department. In most cases there will be a written contract between creditor and bailiff, the purpose of which is to regulate the general administration of enforcement by distress and to ensure that distress is conducted in an acceptable manner.

Magistrate's courts are now required to operate procedures to deal with complaints about the bailiffs that they use and the contract between them should deal with the operation of this and require the firm to have its own procedure. These procedures should be publicised by the court along with the details of the firm's own procedure. Contracts are only awarded by magistrate's courts to bailiffs' firms which have been 'approved'. In deciding whether to approve a firm the courts will check that they have properly trained and controlled staff and have not been taken to court for any unlawful acts or overcharging. Such problems should form the basis of any complaints to a magistrate's court.

Complain to professional associations

All the professional and trade associations representing bailiffs have disciplinary codes and complaints procedures for members that may be turned to for arbitration if attempts to negotiate fail, or as an alternative to them. The use of these procedures is increasingly being built into other complaints schemes, such as in magistrate's courts or in the NSEA.

- *Sheriffs' Officers Association* exists to regulate its members, maintain professional standards and lobby government. It has a disciplinary procedure for dealing with complaints against members. Complaints are handled by a disciplinary committee which will seek the officer's comments and examine his records. They then seek to mediate between the parties. It is possible for an award of compensation to be made and for an officer to be expelled from the Association if the complaint is of sufficient gravity. The Association may be contacted via Ashfield House, Illingworth Street, Ossett West Yorkshire WF5 8AL.

- *Certificated Bailiffs' Association* represents both individual certificated bailiffs and firms. The CBA has a code of practice to which is linked a disciplinary procedure composed of three stages.

1) Complaints should be made on the CBA's complaints form and sent to the Association's Executive Director. The CBA may be contacted at Ridgefield House, 14, John Dalton St., Manchester, M2 6JR or *see www.bailiffs.org.uk*. The complaint will be investigated by the Executive Director who will request information from the member concerned regarding the matters raised in the complaint. The member must respond within 14 days. Based upon the information received, the Executive Director will write to the complainant within 21 days of receiving the complain to state either that:

- he believes the complaint has merit in which case it will be further considered by the Executive Council; or,
- the complaint appears to have no grounds on which to take further action against the member in which case no further action will be taken.

2) If a complaint is heard by the Executive Council, it may impose a penalty on the member (such as a penalty or membership sanction), or it may dismiss the complaint as unfounded.

3) If the complainant is dissatisfied with the Executive Council's decision s/he may apply for the complaint to be

referred to a panel of independent assessors. The Panel's decision is final and will be binding on both parties.

- *Association of Civil Enforcement Agents* exists to represent the employers of bailiffs. It aims to raise standards generally in the industry, a major element in this being the establishment of its complaint procedure.

All Association members have undertaken to abide by the decisions reached at any stage in the complaints procedure and comply with whatever recommendation may be made.

If a complaint is received by a member firm it will initially be handled internally. The complaint will be acknowledged immediately and will be responded to in writing within fourteen days. That reply will be accompanied by the ACEA's leaflet explaining how the Association may become involved to reconsider the matter if the complainant is not satisfied with the firm's response. Certain matters cannot be handled. These are:

- complaints about the amount of the debt/ penalty being collected. This sum was set by the creditor or court and is of course beyond the control of the bailiff firm. Fees are not excluded by this proviso;

- allegations of violence- which should be referred to the police;

- cases already subject to court proceedings. If the complainant has sued, issued replevin or commenced interpleader ACEA will not intervene.

The complainant unhappy with the firm's response may then

complain in writing to the Secretary of the ACEA at Chesham House, 150 Regent St, London W1R 5FA. See also *www.acea.org.uk*. The letter should include details of the complaint, proof of any financial loss suffered and a copy of the firm's reply. This will be acknowledged within three days of receipt and will be sent to three of the Association's directors for their consideration. They will not be connected to the member firm in question. The directors will meet to consider the complaint and may seek further information from the member firm as to its handling of the matter. If it is felt that the problem was not dealt with appropriately a remedy will be proposed (e.g. the return or remission of fees) and the firm will be asked to reconsider its decision. Both parties will be notified of this decision no later than twenty-eight days after the complaint was received.

If the complainant is still not satisfied, s/he may ask that the matter be referred to a panel of independent complaints adjudicators. The panel members are drawn from the likes of local authorities, CAB's and magistrate's courts. Three adjudicators will be asked to sit to consider the complaint, and the aggrieved individual may attend in person to present their case. The offending bailiff or a representative of the firm will also be invited to be present. The ACEA has decided that it will be possible for parties to take along an adviser or other 'McKenziefriend' to assist or support them. If the panel is convinced that the individual's complaint is justified, it may recommend remission, reduction or refund of fees; payment of compensation based on the panel's assessment of the complainant's actual losses or both. Presumably it would also be expected for the member firm in question to issue a formal apology at the same time as any pecuniary restitution. Notice of the decision is sent to the parties. If compensation is being recommended, it will be necessary for the complainant to confirm in writing that s/he accepts this in full and final settlement of the matter. The firm will then be obliged to pay as instructed. The panel's decision is final. If the complainant still is not happy with the result, s/he will have to turn to the other remedies described in this and the next article.

Complaints to Ombudsmen

This remedy may be used where there has been maladministration by a local or central government department which has involved the use of bailiff's services. The aggrieved debtor may complain to the relevant ombudsman e.g.: the Commission for Local Administration for local authorities or the Revenue Adjudicator for the HMRC.

The mal-administration that would form the basis of the complaint includes error, illegal acts and failure to act e.g. neglect and delay, failure to follow proper procedures (such as ignoring a code of practice) or giving misleading (or inadequate) information. If a complaint is upheld following investigation by the ombudsman it is usual for them to recommend review of and improvements to the public body's administration and the award of compensation to the individual.

Bailiff related problems fairly frequently form the basis of complaints to the Local Government Ombudsman, typically arising from poor communications between the council and bailiffs and failure to keep adequate records and accounts.

Court Action

It is always preferable to resolve a complaint informally. It will be easier, quicker and less expensive. However if this route fails a person may always resort to court action, or at least the threat of it. There is a range of remedies available for use in cases of wrongful actions by bailiffs. If the intention is to issue a claim for over £5000, it may be advisable to seek legal advice first, as may also be the case if a more unusual remedy is pursued.

Court action can be taken to find a remedy for "wrongful distress", which can take three forms - illegal, irregular or excessive. Attempts to levy distress can be as wrongful as actual levies, and the same remedies will apply:

- Illegal seizure. An illegality is any act that is forbidden by law. For bailiffs illegality could occur where there is no right to distrain (e.g. the debt has been paid, or its amount tendered) or where an unlawful or unauthorised act is committed during the levy, such as distress at the wrong time, on exempt or third party goods, with forcible entry or when goods not previously seized are removed and sold. Other instances of what would render a distress illegal have been given throughout the text. The effect of showing illegality may be to make the distress both trespass and void from the beginning. Thus showing illegality can both recover the goods seized and damages and also terminate the levy completely. Note that if only some of the goods seized were third parties', and some were the debtor's and available for distress, then the bailiff would not be a trespasser to the house. In such cases it will still be possible to sue for wrongful interference to the goods in question, but the whole levy will not be called into question.

- Irregular seizure: An irregularity is anything done in the wrong manner or without the proper formalities. It may be rectified by the court by the award of damages for the costs caused by it. The validity of the act done is not affected i.e. the distress is not void as with a illegal levy. Thus in bailiffs' law this offence occurs when the levy is correct but subsequent events are not, e.g. selling goods at an undervalue, sale after the debt and costs have been paid or failing to give proper notices. It is more of a technical offence than illegal distress and as the remedy is only the actual damage suffered by the claimant, which may be negligible or difficult to prove depending on the nature of the irregularity, it is often not worth pursuing.

- Excessive seizure. This occurs when more goods are taken than are reasonably required to satisfy the debt and costs. Judging the value of the goods etc must take into account the nature of the forced sale which will have to take place. There will be no basis for a claim if there was only one thing to take, even if its value greatly exceeded the sum due. Because they often fail to appreciate the nature of sale at auction and the prices likely to be raised by the process, plus the natural tendency to overvalue one's own goods, debtors often feel that there has been an excessive levy when there has not. The courts have warned that debtors should expect a generally sceptical reaction to their own estimation of the goods' worth. Consequently it is fair to assume that successful actions for excessive distress will be rare.

The debtor may only employ one remedy at a time.

Suing for damages for illegal distress

Where an illegality has occurred the debtor or owner of the goods seized may sue to recover some compensation, which generally will be either for trespass to land or trespass to goods. It is also possible to sue for trespass to person (i.e. assault and/ or battery) but it may be difficult to prove and less likely to arise. Claims for trespass are made on the same county court form (the Part 7 claim form). The difference will partly be the facts described, but more importantly will be the remedy requested. In claims in respect of trespass to goods, it may be possible to ask for an order for the recovery of the goods.

Trespass to land

Every unlawful entry into or upon property is a trespass for which court action may be taken, even though no actual damage is done. Thus it is trespass for a bailiff to levy illegal distress or to remain on the property after a legal distress has become illegal (e.g. by seizing exempt goods). The fact that the bailiff either had no right to enter or abused a legal right of entry gives the claimant an automatic right to damages.

The action is begun by applying for issue of a county court Part 7 claim form (form N1) seeking damages. Claims may be made against the bailiff who levied and any creditor authorising the illegal act as the bailiff's principal.

The bailiff will receive the claim form with a 'response pack' enabling him to either admit the trespass or to defend the claim. If it is defended it will go to trial at court. How the matter will be heard will depend on the level of damages claimed by the claimant. If he has capped their claim at £5000 the matter will be dealt with as a 'small claim' and will be heard by the more informal process of arbitration. The major advantage to the debtor of this is that if they are unsuccessful, they will not have to meet the defendant's legal costs, though some witness expenses may be payable. If the sum claimed is over £5000, but under £25000, the case will be tried before district judge. If the sum exceeds £25000, trial will be before Circuit Judge. In either case the procedure is more formal and the losing party may expect to pay the other side's legal costs (barrister, solicitors etc.) as well as their own. Legal advice should *always* be sought before making any claim over £5000.

Even if the claim is not defended, and the claimant wins by default, there will still have to be a hearing as the judge will have to hear the details of the case in order to assess the damages that are awarded.

These *general or ordinary damages* may only be nominal. However if specific losses can be shown an additional award of *special damages* may be made to compensate for this. Special damages may cover repairs to detached fixtures or other damage to property; the full value of exempt goods seized and sold; injury to the reputation of business premises; or sums paid to release goods.

Trespass to goods

This is usually referred to as wrongful interference with goods. Wrongful interference may be defined in three ways, though the offences are not completely exclusive and a seizure may turn out to be both conversion and trespass.

- *trespass*: this is direct, intentional or forcible interference with goods. Trespass will arise when there is an illegal seizure and removal. It can also include direct acts causing damage to goods, but the onus of proof of such negligence will be on the claimant (the owner of the goods). The successful claimant is entitled to recover general damages as there has been a trespass.
- *conversion*: includes three different forms of wrongful interference that involve appropriating another's goods or depriving that person of their use. The gist of the claim is that there has been some wrongful act that interferes with or is inconsistent with the owner's rights over their goods.

Wrongfully taking goods into possession will be conversion.

The three forms are:

- wrongful dealing: this is any dealing with or disposal of goods that is inconsistent with the owner's rights. An illegal sale of goods is thus conversion.
- wrongful detention: this covers any detention of goods that deprives a person of the use/possession of them.

- wrongful destruction: this term refers to any negligent loss or destruction that may occur to goods that a bailiff has in possession.

The damages that can be awarded in cases of in conversion are based on the market value of the goods at the date of conversion plus any consequential damages incurred by the claimant e.g. loss of use of a vehicle.

negligence: this is any mishandling of goods leading to their damage. The claim is for the value of the goods lost. The county court action that a person may commence can include an order for the return of the goods (a delivery order), though delivery is only awarded for the recovery of specific and 'irreplaceable' items. The claim will again be issued on the Part 7 claim form. If a claim for damages alone is made, ownership of the goods will be extinguished as the person is implicitly accepting the compensation rather than trying to recover the goods themselves. The details of the case and what is requested- an order for return of the goods, damages (probably of up to £5000), perhaps an injunction (see later) and costs- must be laid out on the claim form or on an attached statement of claim. These claims will require at least one hearing, probably two, to resolve the matter. A procedure similar to an injunction exists for the immediate recovery of goods, but it is rarely used and specialist advice upon it should be taken before any application notice is filed in court.

Injunctions

Injunctions are court orders instructing a person to refrain from doing certain acts (e.g. forcing entry, removing or selling goods) and are available in the county court ancillary to a damages claim (i.e. the court can't grant an injunction alone- there must be at least the basis of a case to sue the bailiff for damages: though the court may not insist that this is followed through once the injunction is made).

Application can be made before the issue of a claim form by the claimant in urgent cases and the court may grant an injunction on terms that a claim is begun in that court. It will be normal for the court to expect the claimant to supply a copy of the statement of claim to be used in the later case, which will request not only that the court make an injunction but also layout the background to the claim for damages.

The applicant must complete form N16A stating the terms of the injunction sought- for instance to prevent forced entry to premises and removal of goods, their sale and any other assault, damage or interference with property. In support an affidavit must be sworn giving the grounds for the application i.e. describing the bailiffs' illegal acts and what further action is threatened. This can be supplied on standard county court form N285.

An application may be made 'ex parte' with only the debtor present at the court, if the District Judge is satisfied that matters are urgent and justify it. Whether or not the court has already made an injunction in an urgent case, there will be a hearing a few days later, typically before Circuit Judge, to decide whether to confirm the terms of the order for a longer period. At this the damages claim will not be tried but there must be evidence of a genuine claim to be heard at a later date. If an injunction is issued it is made on N16 and the bailiff can be committed for breach of an injunction. Application can also be made by requesting an injunction on the Part 7 claim form in a claim for damages. The level of any damages and whether or not to make an injunction will be considered at a hearing,

The courts will take account of several factors when considering applications:

- the parties' legal rights*:* the courts do not favour interfering with the legal right to distrain, so there will have to be both a serious error by the bailiff plus an imminent threat of loss of essential goods, or assault or damage to property, to persuade the court to intervene.

- payment into court*:* the court will not normally make an injunction unless it is satisfied that any person prevented from enforcing a legal claim will be in the same position, in the event that their claim turns out to be right, as if the court had not interfered. The court usually achieves this by making an injunction conditional on the claimant paying all the debt into court; upon which the bailiff is ordered to withdraw. Thus the utility of the injunction is tempered by its possible expense to the claimant.

Damages for irregular distress

The claimant may sue using claim form N1. The instructing creditor can be included in a claim if s/he authorised the distress, though not the irregular act, as the creditor's duty is to ensure proper execution. The debtor can only recover what 'special damages' can be proved. These are based on the *actual* losses suffered, which are often said to be the full value of any goods lost less the debt and costs. In the absence of proof of special damages, the claimant cannot even get a nominal sum. Special damages need to be proved if, for instance, the bailiff sells within five days, sells without appraising or sells without notice of distraint.

Damages for excessive distress

The claim will be conducted as for irregular distress above. The excess will have to be shown to be disproportionate rather than trifling. The price realised at sale is the best evidence of the item's value and will be the basis upon which damages are assessed. A claim can be begun on Part 7 claim form (N1) even when the goods are not yet sold the amount of damages being claimed then being the loss and inconvenience to the debtor occasioned by the goods' removal. If there is no inconvenience as in walking possession, no damages may be awarded. If the distress is both irregular and excessive, damages could be substantial.

Replevin

Replevin is a remedy to obtain recovery of goods that have been illegally seized. It is used rarely because of its obscurity and cost and will, when the provisions of the Tribunals, Courts and Enforcement Act 2007 come into force, be replaced. Replevin applies to statutory distraint as well as to distress for rent. It is not applicable to execution in the High Court. However, the sheriff can be ordered to return wrongfully seized goods. Seizure under the order of a county court or magistrates court cannot normally be replevied unless the warrant in question was issued in excess of or completely outside the court's jurisdiction- both of which will naturally be unlikely though enforcing an invalid order or one that had been cancelled subsequently might be an example. The claim may be brought against the bailiff, the authorising person, c begun in the county court, the powers being found una Sch.1 County Courts Act 1984. Replevin consists of twc

- The replevy The owner presents a notice in the county court (see example- there are no standard forms) stating the facts, provides a replevin bond (security) and gives an undertaking that an action will be commenced within four weeks. The district judge then instructs the court bailiff by warrant to deliver the goods to the owner. The level of security required is set by the district judge at a figure considered sufficient to cover the probable costs of the action and the alleged debt. The owner must then begin the action without delay and undertake to return the goods if ordered.
- The action. A hearing follows with the bailiff as defendant. It will be necessary for the applicant to show that the levy was illegal. If successful, the owner recovers the expenses of the replevy plus damages which are assessed as the value of the replevin bond itself plus any actual damages suffered by reason of the distress. These could be compensation for loss, annoyance and injury to a person's reputation. No further claim could then be made for compensation. If the bailiff is successful, s/he is entitled to an order for the return of the goods and the security is forfeit. Costs may be awarded at the discretion of the court.

Pay the debts and then Sue'

A fairly simple remedy for the debtor could be to pay the debt subject to dispute and then make a county court claim to recover any sums paid on the grounds that they were wrongfully demanded and were paid under duress. Such an action is not an action for damages: all that can be claimed is the sum paid, but no added compensation. Duress in the context of distress means compulsion under which a person pays money to a bailiff through fear of their property (or the property of a close family or household member) being wrongfully seized or detained. The distress in question may be threatened or actual. The payment must not be voluntary, so the debtor should pay the sum claimed under protest. Ideally the person should make the fact that was being made under protest clear in words or in writing, but the court may find that the circumstances of payment or the claimant's conduct are sufficient indication of their intention. Establishing that payment was made under protest is important to the claimant because the general rule is that seizure in a legal distress is **not** duress or illegal pressure and any payment made by the debtor to release goods is simply submission to that form of legal process.

Consequently there must be some wrongful element in the levy and the debtor, in paying, would have to make clear that this was not seen as an end to the matter but simply a way of retaining use of the goods rather than being deprived of them during lengthy litigation over the alleged illegality.

This remedy is commenced by the debtor commencing a Part 7 claim in the county court. This is done by issuing claim form N1 demanding repayment of a specified sum which the defendant bailiff must have received. The claim form has space for the claim to be described in detail. If it is defended the matter will be handled as a small claim where, as is most likely, it is less than £5000.

If no defence is filed, judgment will be entered for the claimant by 'default' and s/he will automatically receive an order to pay the sum claimed without the need for hearing. Electing to sue this way extinguishes any right to damages on the part of the debtor, although it is possible for a claimant to sue for trespass or the money paid on the same claim form.

Certification

A bailiff must hold a county court certificate in order to levy distress for rent, local taxes and road traffic penalties. Many other creditors will prefer to use certificated bailiffs even though this is not mandatory for them.

Again, this is an area that will change when the TCEA 2007 comes into full force. The certificate authorises the holder to levy anywhere in England and Wales during a period of two years. A bailiff may be fined for levying without a certificate. Such distress is also trespass.

Certification offers debtors two benefits:

- some guarantee of the knowledge and suitability of the individual bailiff; and;
- recourse to a procedure to complain about the bailiff through the county court if something goes wrong.

The procedure for granting and revoking certificates is found in the Distress for Rent Rules 1988. The 'issuing' county court can grant a certificate only if it feels that the applicant is a fit and proper person and has an adequate knowledge of the laws of distress. It is fair to say at present that the certification process is not much of a test of an applicant's suitability or knowledge. Each court must compile and display a list of all bailiffs holding certificates on February 1st each year. There is also a central register held by the Court Service which can be consulted by the public- contact the Court Service, South Side, Victoria St, London.

If a complaint to the court is planned, it will be important to check the details of the bailiff through either the local court or through Court Service.

Any complaint as to the conduct or fitness of a bailiff should be made to the court which issued the certificate. A standard complaint form (Form 4) is available from county courts. The court then sends written details to the bailiff who must reply in writing within fourteen days, or a longer period if the court allows. A hearing will be arranged before a Circuit Judge to explain why the certificate should not be cancelled if the bailiff either does not reply or the reply does not satisfy the Judge that the person remains fit to hold a certificate.

The bailiff is informed by notice and the complainant and any other interested party receive a copy. At the hearing the bailiff may attend and make representations, as may the complainant. The procedure is determined by the Judge, including what evidence shall be allowed, and the hearing may proceed even in the bailiff's absence.

After hearing the parties, if the complaint is upheld the Judge may cancel the certificate and/or may order that the security be forfeited either wholly or partly to compensate the complainant, to cover any costs and expenses s/he may have incurred and also to cover the court's own costs, expenses and fees. The court publicises the cancellation both locally and nationally if the bailiff operates outside the district of that county court.

Complaint to magistrate's court

Any person aggrieved by a levy, or an attempt to levy, for local taxes and child support maintenance can appeal to the Magistrates Court. The process is begun by making a 'complaint' on a standard form, giving details of the parties and outlining the case and requesting the issue of a claim form directed to the creditor. This statutory remedy does not take away the person's alternative right to sue for damages or to replevy in the county court. At the hearing, if the court is satisfied that the levy was wrongful, it can order the return of the goods distrained. As an alternative to ordering return of goods the court may order an award of compensation for any goods sold equal to an amount which, in opinion of the court, would be awarded by way of damages for trespass or otherwise in connection with the irregularity. It has been held that the amount of damages that can be awarded can cover all losses caused by the wrongful levy, including damages for annoyance, injury to credit and reputation. The court can also order the creditor and bailiffs to desist from any levying in an irregular manner and so benefits everyone living in an area.

Criminal remedies

- *Violent entry* Section 6 Criminal Law Act 1977 makes it an offence for any person to use or threaten violence, without lawful authority, in order to secure entry into any premises. On conviction a person can be fined up to £5000 and/ or sentenced to up to 6 months in prison. For the entry to be criminal there must be someone on the premises opposed to the entry and the bailiff seeking to enter must know this. The violence may be directed against the premises or person. If such an entry is in progress the police may be called by the debtor and a constable may arrest anyone suspected of committing such an offence.

- *Criminal damage* An illegal violent entry may also involve criminal damage. This offence arises wherever another's property is intentionally or recklessly destroyed or damaged without lawful excuse, or threats to that effect are made. There is no power of arrest by a constable at the time the offence is being committed, as with forced entry and it would be up to the police whether to pursue a prosecution.

In either case if the bailiff does not comply, he faces committal or daily penalties until the goods are returned. The complaint will be on a standard form as in the magistrates appeal described earlier, and will be relatively cheap.

Appendix 1

Sample Interpleader claim

To the District Judge of County Court

TAKE NOTICE that I, of claim the goods and chattels specified below [*or specified in the list attached to this notice*] which have been taken by you at under a warrant of execution against the goods of of as I am given to understand.

The grounds for my claim are as follows:-

Dated the day of x 2008 Signature:

Inventory of goods

Third Party Declaration

To the landlord & bailiff:

1. I the undersigned am the undertenant of [tenant's name] at ***or*** {*am lodger in* ***or*** *am not a tenant or beneficially interested in any tenancy of or of any part of*} the premises known as [address] and occupied by [tenant] {*and my undertenancy is not one to which the Law of Distress Amendment Act 1908 is expressed to apply*}.

2. The said [immediate tenant] has no right of property or beneficial interest in the furniture goods and chattels specified in the annexed inventory and distrained [*or threatened to be distrained*] by you.

3. The said furniture, goods and chattels are my property [*or are in*

my lawful possession] and are not goods to which the Law of Distress Amendment Act 1908 is expressed not to apply.

* [4. There is no rent due from me to the said [tenant's name] ***or*** the sum of £X is due from me to the said [tenant] ***or*** future instalments will become due to him on [date] to the amount of £X.
* [5. I hereby undertake to pay you [or the landlord] the said rent so due or to become due to the said [tenant] until the arrears in respect of which the distress was levied [*or authorised to be levied*] have been paid off.]

Inventory

Date: Signature:

* Only applies to subtenants or lodgers.

Statutory Declaration
(to prove ownership of goods)

I [*name*] of [*address*] do solemnly and sincerely declare that:

[*explain situation regarding ownership of disputed goods and add list of items claimed to be owned by you*].

And I make this solemn declaration conscientiously believing the same to be true, and by virtue of the provisions of the Statutory Declarations Act 1835.

[*signature*]
[*signature of Justice of Peace*]
Justice of the Peace for the County of [specify].

Appendix 2

Statement of claim

IN THE COUNTY COURT
Claim no: XXXXX

Between:

Mr *Claimant*

v

Mayor & Burgesses of the Borough of *1st defendants*

&

Bailiffs *2nd defendants*

<u>Statement of claim</u>

1) The claimant is tenant of ......He is liable for local taxes assessed on the property. In about......the claimant owed the first defendant the sum of.......representing arrears of Community Charge of £ and £.....bailiff's "return fee". The first defendants had instructed the second defendants, as their agents, to levy distraint at the claimant's home. On or about......the claimant agreed with the first defendant that he would pay the sum due at the rate of £... per week and the defendant agreed to withdraw the bailiffs, always provided that the claimant maintained the agreed payments. There were no other arrears of Community Charge then owing.

2) Some instalments were missed and therefore the first defendant

issued a second warrant on…..However the claimant paid the sum outstanding in full by……. This has been acknowledged by the first defendant. The claimant avers that the subsequent attempt to levy distraint was thus rendered illegal.

3) The claimant further avers that the first defendants were negligent in failing to keep proper records of payment and in failing to notify its agents, the second defendants, that the debt had been paid in full and that the warrant should therefore by returned. As a result of this negligence, an illegal attempt to levy distraint took place, by reason of which the claimant suffered loss, damage and inconvenience.

<u>Particulars of Damages</u>

1) Shock and trauma caused by the attempt to levy illegal distraint. This was increased by the fact that the first defendant could not, for the two days following the visit, make contact with their agents to withdraw the warrant.
2) Cost of about twenty-five phone calls, made on and the two subsequent days, by the claimant to the first and second defendants in order to try to prevent removal of goods under the purported levy.

3) Taxi hire of… to attend council offices to collect a letter from the first defendant confirming that payment had been made. This was to be shown to the second defendants should they try to attend to remove goods.

4) On……a Mr……a bailiff employed by the second defendants, attended the claimants property acting or purporting to act under

the authority and instructions of the first defendants. He walked up to the front door of the house and, when it was answered by the claimant's girlfriend, asked for the claimant. When the claimant came to the door he endeavoured to step out and close the door behind himself in order to prevent his dog escaping. He was unable to do this because.......barred the way and continued to stand on the very threshold of the house in an intimidating manner.

The claimant informed the bailiff that the debt was paid. The bailiff did not accept this and was not prepared to wait whilst the claimant found receipts to prove the fact. He initially would not provide details of his own instructions, refusing to inform the claimant when the warrant was issued, what the account number was and to what period the debt related. The discussion soon became heated and aggressive as a result of the bailiff's attitude. In particular he became abusive to the claimant on a personal level. The claimant stated that he would seek a court injunction to bar further distraint. The bailiff replied "Don't get funny with me mate". He then returned to his van, which was parked in the street outside the claimant's home.

The claimant then had an opportunity to search for the payment receipts issued by the first defendant. When he located these he took them out to the bailiff who was still sitting in his vehicle outside. On seeing the proof of payment the bailiff once again became very angry and agitated and began shouting. He then left threatening to return on......to remove the claimant's vintage motorcar.

5) By reason of the matters aforesaid the claimant suffered shock, fear, and humiliation and shame in public.

Particulars of Damages

1) The claimant felt threatened and feared that violence would be used against him by the bailiff if he argued too much.

2) The claimant felt intimidated by the bailiff's physical demeanour and approach.

3) The claimant has a heart condition. He was fearful that this would be aggravated by the stress of the incident.

4) The claimant was shocked by the incident and physically shook for some hours afterwards. He also experienced angina attacks for several days afterwards.

5) The claimant's girlfriend, children and neighbours witnessed the scene and this increased his distress and embarrassment.

6) Further by virtue of s69 County Courts Act 1984 the claimant is entitled to recover and claim interest on the amount found to be due at such rate and for such period as the court shall think fit.

7) The claimant states that, in accordance with Order 6 rule 1A County Court Rules 1981, the value of this claim does not exceed £3000.

AND the claimant claims:

1) DAMAGES for illegal distress;

2) DAMAGES for assault;

[*3) AN INJUNCTION to prevent the second defendant's return or removal of goods*]

3) INTEREST thereon, and

4) COSTS.

Dated this….. day of …… 2008.

Signed:

To the District Judge and to the defendants.

Replevin Notice

To the District Judge of…….
County Court,

TAKE NOTICE that I intend to replevy the goods illegally distrained by……. On ………

AND TAKE NOTICE that I intend to commence an action of replevin in the…… County Court in which I will be the claimant and……. Borough Council and ……Bailiffs will be the defendants.

I apply for security to be fixed for the due prosecution of the proposed action.

Dated the day of 2008. Signature

Statement of claim in action of replevin

To the District Judge of County Court

Give statement of events in numbered paragraphs,
1)
2)
describing how distraint was illegal, that replevin was issued & *making claim for damages;*

3) The claimant has suffered loss, damage and injury as a result of the levy of illegal distraint.

Particulars of damage
1) Describe losses &
2) Make claim for costs of replevin

4) The claimant is entitled under s35A Supreme Courts Act to claim interest on the amounts found due at such rate and for such period as the court thinks fit.

AND the claimant claims:
1) DAMAGES for illegal distress;

2) COSTS

3) A DECLARATION that the distraint was illegal and cancellation of the replevin bond.

Signed:

Magistrates Court Appeal

Date:
Magistrates Court

Defendants: London Borough of Bailiffs

Address:

Matter of complaint: An appeal by an aggrieved council tax payer under reg.46 Council Tax (Administration & Enforcement) Regs 1992 [*or reg 15 Non Domestic Rating (Collection & Enforcement) (Local Lists) Regs 1989, or reg 31 Child Support (Collection & Enforcement) Regs 1992*] following an illegal levy of distress by the defendants.

The complaint of: A debtor

Address:

who, upon oath, states that the defendants were responsible for the matter of complaint of which particulars are given above.

Taken & sworn before me

.... Justice of the Peace

....Justices Clerk

Glossary

Bailiff: any official employed to seize goods to recover debt

Close possession: impounding where the bailiff remains at the premises guarding the goods.

Distrain: a verb meaning the act of seizing goods.

Distraint: has the same meaning as distress.

Distress: any summary remedy involving seizure of goods outside the civil courts. In addition, distress can mean the process of entry, seizure and impounding (including possible removal) and can mean the goods seized, the actual subject of the distress.

Excessive distress: distress where more than is required is taken.

Execution: seizure of goods to enforce a civil court judgment. Also, the act of enforcing a warrant to seize goods.

Illegal distress: distress where there is no right to distrain or where a seizure error is committed by the bailiff.

Impounding: the act of securing seized goods so that they have legal protection.

Interpleader: a remedy for third parties to recover wrongly seized goods.

Irregular distress: distress where there is a technical error by the bailiff.

Levy: this word is often interchangeable with the verbs 'distrain', 'seize' and 'execute (a warrant)'. Strictly it refers to the entire process from entry to sale, but commonly it is applied to the process of seizure and impounding.

NSEA: the National Standards for Enforcement Agents (see chapter 1).

Possession: this is now largely interchangeable with 'impounding' and means the process of securing seized goods.

Poundbreach: wrongful interference with impounded goods, by the debtor or a third party.

Replevin: a remedy to recover goods illegally distrained.

Removal: the act of taking seized goods away from the debtor's premises preparatory to sale.

Rescue: self help recovery of seized goods. It may be an offence.

Seizure: identifying goods to the value of the debt being collected.

Sheriff/ sheriff's officer: the High Court bailiff.
Taxation: review and assessment of a bailiff's bill by the county court.

Walking possession: impounding where the bailiff leaves the goods at the debtor's premises under an agreement that they are seized.

Wrongful distress: any distress where an error is made by the bailiff.

Index

Law

A Straightforward Guide to:

Consumer Rights
Bankruptcy Insolvency and the Law
Employment Law
Private Tenants Rights
Family law
Small Claims in the County Court
Contract law
Intellectual Property and the law
Divorce and the law
Leaseholders Rights
The Process of Conveyancing
Knowing Your Rights and Using the Courts
Producing Your own Will
Housing Rights
The Bailiff the law and You
Probate and The Law
Company law
What to Expect When You Go to Court
Guide to Competition Law
Give me Your Money-Guide to Effective Debt Collection
Caring for a Disabled Child

General titles

Letting Property for Profit
Buying, Selling and Renting property
Buying a Home in England and France
Bookkeeping and Accounts for Small Business

Creative Writing
Freelance Writing
Writing Your own Life Story
Writing performance Poetry
Writing Romantic Fiction
Speech Writing

Teaching Your Child to Read and write
Teaching Your Child to Swim
Raising a Child-The Early Years

Creating a Successful Commercial Website
The Straightforward Business Plan
The Straightforward C.V.
Successful Public Speaking

Handling Bereavement
Play the Game-A Compendium of Rules
Individual and Personal Finance
Understanding Mental Illness
The Two Minute Message
Guide to Self Defence
Buying a Used Car
Tiling for Beginners

Go to:

www.straightforwardco.co.uk